REVISED, ENLARGED EDITION

VIC DUNAWAY'S
Complete Book of
BAITS, RIGS AND TACKLE

Also From Florida Sportsman:

**Sport Fish of Florida
Sport Fish of the Gulf of Mexico
Fishing Planner
Best of Waterfront View**

**Florida Sportsman Magazine
Florida Sportsman Fishing Charts
Lawstick Law Guides**

VIC DUNAWAY'S COMPLETE BOOK OF

Baits Rigs & Tackle

Freshwater/Saltwater

By Vic Dunaway

Chief Illustrator
Dan Dunaway

FS BOOKS

Published by Florida Sportsman Magazine
2700 S. Kanner Hwy.
Stuart, FL 34994
www.floridasportsman.com/books

Every Angler's "Must Have" Book...

This book is a comprehensively revised and expanded edition of the all-time best-selling reference book for all kinds of fishing.

Ever since its first edition two decades ago, *Vic Dunaway's Complete Book of Baits, Rigs and Tackle* has established itself as the one book covering all the key mechanics that are so important to fishing success at every level of interest or experience, from pole-fishing to big-game angling.

And now, BRT—as it is nicknamed—is bigger and more comprehensive than ever.

Every angler, whether a beginner or expert, whether in fresh water or salt, will want to own this valuable volume of know-how and refer to it often over the fun-filled fishing years ahead.

In these pages you'll find the same authoritative yet easily understood information that caused the record-setting sales success of the book's first eleven printings that have served more than a quarter of a million delighted BRT buyers.

It's a remake of a classic with stores of new information, illustrations and tips that will keep you up to date on all the latest advancements in tackle, equipment and expertise.

So enjoy a classic revisited. And hook a big one for Vic.

Karl Wickstrom

Publisher

TABLE OF CONTENTS

CONTENTS / continued

Chapter 1

Baits, Rigs & Tackle

Rods and Reels

Spinning

Open-face spinning outfits are by far the most versatile of fishing tackle. These rigs are available in a wide array of sizes suitable for everything from panfishing with 2-pound-test line to heavy-duty ocean trolling or surf casting with lines testing 20 or 25 pounds.

How does spinning tackle differ from so-called "conventional" tackle? Basically, the only difference is in how the reel operates. A spinning reel has a fixed spool which never revolves during the cast or retrieve. Line is retrieved by a pickup mechanism (bail) which revolves around the spool as you turn the crank, thus wrapping line onto the spool. When you cast, you fold this bail out of the way, and

Spin tackle handles a variety of lures.

line simply slips off the end of the spool.

By contrast, a "conventional" or revolving-spool reel is designed so that the spool turns when you turn the crank. The spool also revolves during the cast.

This basic difference accounts for the rapid rise in popularity of spinning tackle since its introduction to this country shortly after World War II. Because the spinning reel spool did not revolve, it immediately eliminated the beginning fisherman's chief bugaboo, the backlash. When you cast with a revolving-spool reel, the spool often gets to turning faster than the flying lure. Unless this tendency is corrected with careful light pressure of the thumb, or a mechanical device in the reel, such as a magnet, the over-running spool causes a bad tangle of line, called a backlash.

Since a spinning reel spool does not revolve at all, there is no possibility of an over-run, hence no possibility of a backlash. The beginner can pick up a spinning outfit and, with only a minute's instruction on how to hold the line and fold back the bail, can begin to cast at once without fear of backlash. He won't cast very well, of course, and will still need to practice for distance, accuracy and trajectory. But at least he's in business, fast.

Let it be plainly said, however, that spin-fishing is not free of tangles. Tangles do develop often in spinning lines but they are not caused by backlash. Spinning tangles are usually the result of twisted line or loosely-wrapped line, or a combination of both. They can be minimized by the attentive angler.

Here are some other characteristics of open-faced spinning tackle, that set it apart from conventional gear: The reel is mounted on the underside of the rod, by means of a reel-mount (foot) several inches long. Naturally, the rod guides are also on the underside of the rod, and extend farther out from the shaft than do conventional guides. Spinning guides, too, are larger in diameter.

The fisherman grips the spinning outfit with his right hand (assuming a right-handed person, of course), by straddling the reel foot—two fingers in front of the foot; two fingers behind. The rod stays in his right hand throughout his fishing. He cranks with his left hand. When using a conventional outfit, the routine is to cast with the right hand, then swap hands and also crank with the right hand.

With all the advantages named, will spinning someday completely replace conventional tackle?

Definitely not. There are certain fishing specialties where conventional gear is a must, and numerous specialties for which spinning tackle can be used, but not as efficiently as conventional gear.

For instance, even the heaviest spinning gear is not suited for lines larger than 30-pound test, at the most. The majority of spinning experts place the practical limit at 20-pound line.

Even in fresh water, a conventional outfit (in this case baitcasting tackle) is superior to spinning when you make frequent use of large topwater plugs or heavy lures of any kind (five-eighths of an ounce and up), or when you fish with lines testing 15 pounds or more. Small freshwater spinning reels do not handle springy 15-pound line at all well. And a larger spinning reel, capable of handling the heavy line, simply isn't comfortable for steady freshwater casting. Again, you can make-do with spinning tackle, but not so satisfactorily.

On the other end of the scale, however, baitcasting tackle is of lit-

A nifty array of baitcasting outfits.

tle use for tossing lures under one-fourth of an ounce. And the plug reel's light-line limit (except in the hands of a few experts) is 6-pound-test. Ultra-light spinning can handle lines as skimpy as 2-pound-test, and lures that seem almost weightless.

SPINNING RODS

Spinning rods range in length from as short as 4 feet or so (ultra-light), to as much as 11 or 12 feet (surf spinning). The two most popular lengths for general angling are 6.5 and 7 feet. Tubular fiberglass was for many years the most popular rod material and still is strongly represented in the marketplace, but graphite currently is more prominent. Actually, composites of graphite with fiberglass and perhaps other materials, such as Kevlar, account for most of the rod blanks made today.

Costlier than glass, graphite is lighter, yet does more "work" with less arc of the rod. Also, it delivers more "feel" of lure action

Light spinning rod butt

Two-hand spinning

Surf spinning

and of nibbles or strikes. Providing more power with less weight, the appeal of graphite is strong. Graphite rods are beautiful to handle and more efficient than glass in putting the pressure on hooked fish.

Modern fiberglass blanks, however, are lighter and stronger than they used to be. They also are more "forgiving" and can withstand more accidental abuse than high-content graphite rods. Glass rods (and glass-graphite composites) continue in high favor among salt-water anglers, and for certain freshwater specialties, such as crankbait fishing for bass, where the yielding or "forgiving" qualities of the glass blank helps prevent the hooks of a crankbait from being torn from the bass's mouth.

For all-around light spinning, choose a 6.5- or 7-foot rod. The usual range of line sizes in this category is 6- to 12-pound-test, and the usual range of lure or sinker weights is one-eighth to perhaps five-eighths of an ounce.

Unfortunately, there is no standard way to define rod action, but most rods are marked by the manufacturer with a range of suitable line sizes and lure weights. You can let this clue your choice. If one rod is marked, say, for "8-15 pound line" and another for "4-10 pound line" you could use 8-pound with either, but the angler who wants a stouter action for such work as bassing or saltwater fishing would choose the former, whereas the light-lure/light-line specialists would pick the latter. You should lean toward the lighter action (that is, considerable whippiness) if you use 6- or 8-pound line in fresh water or in salt water for relatively small, shallow-water species. Look for stouter actions (still with considerable flex for casting, but more rigid in the butt half of the blank) if you use 10 or 12-pound line and need to cast heavier lures, or if you do some horsing or lifting in your chosen type of fishing.

Spinning rods designed especially for going after largemouth bass are exceptions to the "6.5 or 7-foot" rule. These may be only 5.5 or 6 feet long but still with heavy or medium-heavy actions. Their shorter length is dictated partly by the storage limitations of many bass boats. Some casting distance is lost when you use a relatively short, stiff rod, but bassers generally use heavier lures and this makes up for it.

Bass spinning rods also make a good choice for some saltwater fishing, such as vertical jigging from a boat, where casting distance isn't important but fighting ability is. Actions being roughly equal, a short rod has more lifting power than a longer one.

The next category is called intermediate. Rods range in length from seven feet to nine but vary a great deal in action. East Coast saltwater anglers often like a pretty stout tip and plenty of beef throughout, since they use their intermediate rods for tough inshore species such as striped bass, bluefish and snook. And they use the same gear for much offshore fishing too. On the other hand, West-Coast and Great Lakes fishermen whose main fishing diet is salmon or steelhead, prefer a fast-taper rod design with quite a light tip, but plenty of "backbone" in the butt section.

Moving on, we come to a category of 7.5- to 9-foot rods, used mainly with lines testing 10 to 20 pounds. Rod action is considerably heavier than for the intermediate category—not necessarily because stouter lines are used, but because a rugged rod is needed for utmost power in fighting big fish, and because lure or terminal-rig weights may be much heavier. Spinning tackle in this class should be chosen for most offshore fishing, and some inshore fishing where water is deep and big fish are expected.

A similar category is surf spinning tackle, with rods running 9 to 12 feet in length. The obvious advantage of such length is to power out long casts in the surf. But the long rods are also useful in pier, jetty and bridge fishing, and on open party boats, for casting live baits.

Note that the categories defined are general classifications and that there is much overlapping of usefulness.

Here are some quality features to look for in spinning rods:

1. Reel Seats. These should be of screw-locking design and corrosion-resistant material. Graphite is widely used, even in relatively low-price rods and certainly is the most corrosion-free and trouble-free. When rod shopping, be very sure to borrow a reel from the store's display (or try the one you plan to buy) and mount it on the rod. Then grip the outfit in your usual way and go through some casting motions. There are a great many reel seat designs these days and you want to be sure that what you buy feels comfortable.

2. Guides. Those with interior rings of aluminum oxide and other high-tech ceramic materials are extremely smooth and hard, thus virtually eliminating severe line fray. Stainless steel rings are also very good, and proven in years of use. They will groove from heavy wear, but few anglers fish hard enough for this to be a problem. Still, all guides should be checked frequently for signs of wear or damage. Stainless steel guides are often chosen for ultra-light and super-light rods because of their lighter weight. Light weight is also the reason why so many single-footed guides are seen on today's rods. Obviously, however, they cannot provide the same support as traditional double-foot guides, which should be chosen for all heavy-duty demands.

3. Wraps. The double-wrap is traditionally the most solid method of fixing guides to the rod blank. Under each guide there is a wrap

Good line roller helps spot a quality reel.

of thread. The feet of the guide are placed on the underwrap, and another wrap is made, usually with thread of contrasting color. Single wraps—winding the guide feet directly on the rod shaft—are found these days on many top-quality rods and are reliable because of the strength provided by epoxy finishes. Double wraps are often used on custom or high-end rods for sheer decoration.

4. Finish. Some low-priced rods are simply dipped in varnish. This provides a suitable finish but not a long-lasting one. Epoxy finishes, or finishes of other tough modern coatings, are widely used by the top tackle manufacturers, even on many of their lower-priced models. All quality rods will show you a gleaming coat of tough, modern material, and on the most carefully-made ones the finish is so thick and glass-smooth that the wraps underneath cannot be felt by your fingers.

5. Decorative wraps. Intricate decorative wraps, such as the diamond or variations, have no functional purpose, but add much to the rod's appearance and are important to many discriminating anglers. Anyway, such wraps are indicative of the rod's overall quality.

ONE-PIECE ROD OR TWO-PIECE? By and large, a two-piece rod—or even a three- or four-piece "travel rod"—is not significantly weaker, for most practical fishing purposes, than a one-piece. And the takedown feature, obviously, is appealing for ease of transportation. The old headache of the metal ferrule, which often corroded and involuntarily made a one-piece rod of a two-piece one, is just about gone. Butt and tip sections of nearly all rods today fit together without a ferrule, glass-over-glass or graphite-over-graphite. Some fishermen, mostly saltwater veterans, still prefer one-piece spinning rods, and with reasonable cause. While it's true that two-piece rods are not apt to fail at the joint in most fishing, it could happen in a prolonged fight with a rugged fish, especially if the rod is in the hands of an experienced light-tackle angler who's in the habit of putting, and keeping, maximum strain on the rod. Under such conditions, a one-piece rod definitely is stronger, and fishermen who need such strength are more than willing to put up with the inconvenience of a stick that can't be taken down.

One more word about rod actions. You will hear the terms "fast taper" and "regular taper" often used in describing spinning rods (fly and plug rods too). A fast taper rod is one in which the diameter of the blank at the butt end is quite large. The whole blank tapers with obvious abruptness from the broad butt section to the slender tip. In rods of regular taper (also called slow action or parabolic), the variation in diameter of the blank is more gradual from butt to tip.

In a fast taper rod, the butt section is virtually rigid; all casting action is provided by the limber tip. A regular taper, or rod has some action throughout its length. The fast taper rod, as hinted earlier, is a favorite among steelhead and trout spinfishermen, and among anglers on Pacific Coast party boats, who need the delicate tip for casting fragile live baits.

15

Unfortunately, the terms fast taper or regular taper do not indicate how light or heavy a particular rod's action may be. Either style can be obtained in a wide range of strengths, and some fast-taper rods have very stout tips.

SPINNING REELS

Spinning reels are functionally the same, regardless of size, and the basic reason there are different sizes is so the angler can select a reel which will accommodate a suitable quantity of the size line he plans to use.

Though this isn't critical for most fishing, particularly fresh water, a convenient rule of thumb to follow in choosing the size spinning reel for your own purposes, is to buy one that holds at least 200 yards of the heaviest line you intend to use; 300 yards if you use your spinning outfit to take on big, long-running fish.

Matching reel size to line size is important from other stand-

Spinning reel

Rear-drag spinning reel

points too—spool diameter, overall weight of your outfit and sometimes line economy. Perhaps you could get enough 15-pound line on an ultra-light reel to serve your purposes, but line so heavy and springy won't behave on the narrow ultra-light spool. Much better to move up to a reel with wider diameter. On the other side of the coin, why use 8-pound line on, say, an intermediate size reel? You'd have to pack the spool with far more line than you'd expect to use, and the weight of the larger reel would get unnecessarily cumbersome.

It must be noted, however, that anglers seeking big offshore fish with light spinning lines generally choose larger reels because of the greater capacity—and also because of the larger-diameter spool, which makes for more efficient drag.

For whatever reasons, various sizes of spinning reels are needed to cover all applications. For quick review, let's divide them into the following groups, although there are slight size variations within the groups—what with so many manufacturers turning out so many different models.

MINI-SYSTEMS—Here are the tiniest of spinning reels. They're little jewels that sit on wispy rods. Obviously, mini-systems turn baby fish into brawny ones, thus increasing fun. But mini-outfits also can be used on bass and larger fish in open water, where they have the advantage of being able to present seemingly weightless lures to fish that may have become leery of large offerings. Mini reels work best with lines testing one to four pounds

ULTRA LIGHT—These are the smallest reels in popular use. They can be used with the same line sizes as the minis and, although a bit heavier, their larger spools provide more capacity and faster line pickup. Average capacity is about 200 yards of four-pound line.

STANDARD—These are light reels in the most commonly used size range. The approximate capacity is 200 yards of 10-pound line and this size is ideal for lines of anywhere from 6- to 12-pound test.

INTERMEDIATE—A popular size for coastal fishing and, in fresh water for salmon, muskie, landlocked stripers and other large fish. Approximate capacity is 200-250 yards of 15-pound line. Frequently used with 10- or 12-pound when extra capacity is needed.

HEAVY—There are now a lot of big spinning reels and you should be able to find the size you need to handle a healthy amount of any line from 12- to 30-pound test.

In addition to size, you should consider design and quality in selecting spinning reels. Skirted spool reels constitute the most popular design and are offered in a staggering number of models by all the major manufacturers and many smaller ones.

The skirted spool minimizes the chance that line will creep beneath the spool and get tangled in the shaft. Most skirted-spool reels also allow you to work the bail either automatically (by turning the crank) or with your hand. In addition, the spool skirt can be easily snubbed by hand to provide extra drag pressure in spot situations

Other features to check for in buying a spinning reel:

1. Ballbearing action. Not essential, but very desirable for greater ease in cranking and for dependability and reduced wear at critical mechanical points. The best spinning reels will have ballbearings at several critical points.

2. Construction and finish. Housings should be of graphite or anodized aluminum. Most nowadays are of graphite, as are the reel spools. Reels with anodized aluminum spools are probably the best choice for large spinning reels and reels that will get a lot of heavy work in salt water.

3. Bail. Should be of heavy stainless steel wire and should click solidly into open position and snap back sharply.

17

In skirted spool reels you will find a choice between internal trip mechanisms for closing the bail, and a setup that simply knocks the bail closed when it hits an external projection on the reel mount. Both systems usually allow you to close the bail either by cranking the handle or by manipulating the bail wire with your hand. Some anglers prefer the internal trip because it is quieter and closes more easily than the external device, especially if you don't turn the handle sharply when starting your retrieve. The external trip, however, is good because a bail using this device seldom goes out of whack and needs repair.

4. Line roller. This should revolve easily to minimize line wear and should be of hardened, corrosion-resistant material. Those with internal bushings are less likely to freeze, but keep all rollers well maintained and lightly oiled.

5. Drag. A positive, smooth-working drag is a necessity for spinning reels because of the light and easily broken lines that are used. The most satisfactory type of drag available on spinning reels today is the "front drag" featuring a multiple-disc setup inside the spool. Drag is adjusted simply by turning the front cap. The discs (washers) are alternately hard and soft—the hard ones being of stainless steel and the soft ones of composite synthetic material, leather, Teflon, felt, or some combination of those. The soft washers, with the exception of Teflon, should be kept lightly oiled. Also, drags will work far more smoothly if all pressure is backed off of them after the day's fishing.

Many spinning reels have "rear drags" which are adjusted by means of a dial at the back of the gear housing. This type of drag is far less efficient because it is more difficult to service and maintain and because heat cannot dissipate very easily from the washers, which are inside the gear housing. Rear drags are fine on light reels, but should be avoided for heavy-duty applications.

CLOSED FACE SPINNING

Closed-face spinning tackle (also called push-button or spincast) is a marriage of the spinning reel and baitcasting rod. This tackle is extremely popular in all freshwater areas, but not well suited to saltwater fishing, although it is sometimes used.

The spinning reel, in this case, is of modified design and looks entirely different from an open-face reel—but a spinning reel it is, nevertheless. The spool is fixed and does not revolve during cast and retrieve.

A closed-face spinning reel is easily identified by the cone which covers the spool. There is a narrow aperture at the small end of the cone, through which the line slips. There is a large push-button at the rear of the reel, with which the angler controls his cast.

To cast, you merely push the button with your thumb, and hold the button in depressed position until the moment you wish to release the line. Then you merely lift your thumb from the button and the cast is underway.

The reel mounts on the top side of the rod-handle in the same

Closed-face reel

way as you would mount a baitcasting reel. And any baitcasting rod can be used. Experience has shown, however, that reasonably light-action rods, 6 or 6.5 feet long, provide the most satisfactory casting results with a closed-face reel.

As you can see, the push-button system is even easier for a beginner to use than open-face spinning. In addition, the closed-face has been welcomed with open arms by many folks who were accustomed to revolving-spool outfits, and who were reluctant to try open-face spinning because the operational mechanics of casting were somewhat different.

All closed-face reels are sold with spools pre-filled, usually with 6- or 8-pound line, although some of the larger models are loaded with line as heavy as 15- or 20-pound. Naturally, you should use a stouter rod with the larger reels and heavier lines.

Counterparts of the tiny mini-systems described in the spinning section are available in spin-cast tackle, and just as pleasant to use.

Closed-face spinning tackle is entirely adequate for every phase of freshwater fishing. One disadvantage, compared to open-face spinning is that line problems are hidden and more difficult to clear. Another is that the line cannot easily be controlled (feathered) after the cast is underway. Therefore, accuracy suffers. But with enough practice you can become pretty darned accurate with the closed-face reel nevertheless.

Saltwater fishing is another story. Here, even the large closed-face reels are at a definite disadvantage because of limited line capacity. And closed-face reels also require an extra measure of cleaning and preventive maintenance to keep them operative in a salty environment.

All closed-face reels have adjustable drags and many are very good, but none are likely to be as silky-smooth and reliable as the front drags on top-quality open-face reels.

Bass are big pets of baitcasters.

BAITCASTING TACKLE

"Baitcasting" refers to a fishing system that makes use of small revolving-spool reels, most of which are equipped with level-wind mechanisms.

During the early days of spinning's popularity boom following World War II, it was widely predicted that baitcasting would fade entirely from the angling scene, and for a time the system did go into a sharp decline in popularity. But the ranks are now larger and more avid than ever, and increasing all the time. Today, baitcasting is the workhorse tackle of American bass fishing, just as it was in the first half of the century, before spinning arrived on our shores. It is very popular too, of course, for other kinds of freshwater and saltwater fishing.

The rejuvenation has been due to the development of modern reels that offer a combination of free-spool casting, dependable adjustable drags, anti-backlash aids and other features. Casting rods have developed apace with the reels to provide baitcasting with a range of versatility that the old-time bass fisherman never dreamed of.

"Backlash" is the scare word for a lot of people who might like to take up baitcasting, but who fear the snarled-up consequences of improper casting technique. It's true that backlashes will occur frequently while you're learning to cast (and occasionally after you become proficient). But take heart in the knowledge that once you do learn to cast well you will enjoy even more freedom from line problems than with spinning tackle—thanks to inherently less line twist.

As mentioned, modern reels help make your learning task easier because of their anti-backlash devices. These take the form, usually, of either a centrifugal mechanism or a set of magnets in the spool housing that slow the spool to help prevent over-running. Both types allow you to adjust the tension by means of a screw on the reel's end cap. Of course, the higher you set the tension, the shorter your cast will be. These devices are of definite help to the beginner and occasional fisherman, but as your experience grows and your "thumbing" becomes more refined, the mechanical spool tension should be gradually eased back, until finally you use little or none of it.

This may surprise you: In cases where rod action, line size and lure weight are similar for both outfits, baitcasting tackle is capable of delivering considerably longer casts than spinning tackle.

The outfit is also superior to spinning for accurate, short-range casting—particularly with large lures.

BAITCASTING RODS

The traditional baitcasting rod features an offset reel seat with a short, one-hand grip and an even shorter foregrip. Once, nearly every baitcasting rod of this design had a removable handle—the blank being fitted to a separate grip assembly. Good modern rods, however, feature through-blank construction, meaning that the shaft extends the full length of the grip. Not only did this bring a huge improvement in strength but also in sensitivity. By far, the most popular lengths for one-hand baitcasting rods are 5, 5.5 and 6 feet.

There is another major "family" of baitcasting rods—those with extra-long butts for two-handed casting and fighting. These also are of through-blank construction and usually have substantial foregrips that are of great help in tussling big fish. This style of butt got its start in coastal waters, where it was used on sticks known as "popping rods," but has long since been embraced by many freshwater fishermen, especially bass anglers and pursuers of steelhead and salmon.

Two-handed rods are offered in a huge variety of lengths and actions, from as short as 4.5 and 5 feet to 7 or 7.5 feet. Saltwater fishermen in general lean toward heavy-action baitcasting rods, but bassers like their rods stout too.

Baitcasting: pistol grip

Baitcasting: two-hand or flipping grip

Flipping rods are a common example of this design.

As in spinning, Great Lakes and West Coast salmon and trout anglers lean toward much lighter actions and greater length. Flipping rods are long too—7 or 7.5 feet, usually—and many have telescoping butts that reduces the length by a foot or more for easier storing and transporting.

BAITCASTING REELS

As previously mentioned, modern baitcasting reels feature free-spool casting capability and adjustable drag. On some reels, the level-wind continues to operate during the cast; on others, the free-spool button also deactivates the level wind. This theoretically increases casting distance because the line does not have to "follow" the level wind while it's going out.

In practice, however, this is not necessarily so because friction may be increased during the cast by line leaving one end of the spool and exiting through the stationary level wind at the other.

Some reels offer an optional anti-reverse, sometimes called a "flipping switch", which allows the handles to rotate backward in the manner of baitcasting reels of another era. This allows small amounts of line to be let off the reel by cranking backward—a convenience in flipping. For casting, the switch is thrown to engage the anti-reverse once more and thus allow the gears to disengage and the spool to spin freely during the cast.

Although there are many, many models of free-spool baitcasting reels, you might notice two rough "families" that differ slightly in basic design. First, there is a group with round end plates, a design featured by the very first of the post-war, free-spool baitcasting reels. Often referred to as "round" reels, they feature greater line capacity than the other basic design (which we will talk about in a minute) plus metal spools and mostly metallic construction. Of all true baitcasting reels, the "round" ones are best suited for salt water and for long-running species in fresh water. They typically feature the centrifugal type of anti-backlash protection and most

"Round" baitcasting reel

Light baitcasting reel

have a clicker button that can be engaged to provide a warning noise when line is leaving the disengaged spool, as in live-bait fishing.

Round reels come in two basic sizes—one holding about 200 yards of 10-pound line and the other about 200 yards of 15- or 17-pound. The different capacity is accounted for by a longer spool in the larger model; all other components are the same (except that the pillars must be longer too, of course). Even larger sizes are available in this design, but purists don't think they really qualify for the "baitcasting" category.

The principal disadvantage of the "round" reels is their weight, and this probably is what led to the development of early models in the other family of reels—those identifiable by their generally smaller size, elliptical end plates and the use of graphite material, wherever practical, to cut down weight. Another characteristic of these reels is that their spools are made light and small to increase casting efficiency and distance. Since bass anglers make up the huge majority of this market, line capacity is of little concern. There are some large-capacity models in this category, of course, but few, if any, can match the "round reels" when it comes to packing on a lot of line.

Close manufacturing tolerances allow all the major brands and models of today's baitcasting reels to be used with monofilament lines and most of them are. Braided nylon line, the standard for baitcasting many years ago, is seldom seen any more, but a new generation of ultra-strong, ultra-thin braids has arrived upon the scene to challenge monofilament's domination. More about this can be found in the section on Fishing Lines.

FLYFISHING TACKLE

Almost every angler who has made a reasonable try at flycasting considers this system the ultimate in sportfishing satisfaction and enjoyment. Even more than that, it is often the best way to put meat on the table—especially when that meat is a mess of panfish or stream trout.

In a few situations, and for certain fish, fly tackle produces more strikes in salt water, too: however, saltwater flyrodders seldom look upon their chosen sport as a better way to catch fish, but as a more challenging and satisfying way.

Some folks shy away from flycasting because it seems to them an almost magical style of angling that defies their own capabilities. But really, flycasting basics are almost as easy to learn as spinning, and with only a couple of short practice sessions virtually anyone can begin using the fly with effect for bass and panfish.

On the other hand, flyrodding does leave more room for improvement, refinement and development of special abilities than any other system. If you wish, you can progress from panfish and bass fishing (after developing a variety of flyfishing skills in both) to going after trout, steelhead, salmon and all sorts of specialized saltwater targets.

If you are unfamiliar with even the broad concept of how flycasting works, here is a brief explanation: In other forms of casting, the weight of the lure carries out your line. In flyfishing, all the casting weight is distributed over the working length of the flyline itself; flies and flyrod lures are, for practical purposes, weightless.

As you can now guess, flycasting requires completely different timing from spinning or baitcasting; you have to make your backcast with 20 or 30 feet of line protruding from the end of the rod. That's why spin and plug fishermen may have a hard time learning to cast a fly. The problem doesn't really lie in learning how to flycast, but in unlearning the techniques and timing they use with spinning and baitcasting tackle.

A beginner who has never used any kind of gear usually masters his flycasting basics without the least bit of trouble.

Numerous good books on flycasting are available, and the line manufacturers offer pamphlets of instruction. It is indeed possible to learn from the printed word. But it is many times easier to learn through personal teaching. If you have friends who are proficient in flycasting they can be of great help, but they may not be able to spot flaws in timing or stroke that are holding back your progress. If you are serious about learning to flycast, or about improving enough to take on the more challenging kinds of fishing, then the expense of lessons or schools conducted by professionals will be money well spent.

In selecting fly tackle, balance between rod action and line weight is of paramount importance. As we will see in the following discussions, the task is not overly difficult anymore, because rods are marked with recommended line weights, and because a standard system of nomenclature for designating weight and design of flylines is used by all major manufacturers.

FLYRODS

Most flyrods today are made of graphite of one sort or another, although many glass rods and graphite-glass composites are avail-

Flyrod grip

able too. Split bamboo remains in favor among a few traditionalists. Regardless of materials, the common range of lengths in this country is from 7 feet to 9.5 feet.

Graphite rods are sold at several different price levels. Some very good ones of 100% graphite (or close) are offered at reasonable prices by most full-line rod manufacturers, as well as by specialty flyrod houses. The latter, however, can also show you rods costing several times as much, the difference being in advanced graphite formulas, combined with superior finish and cosmetics. Needless to say, beginners should stick to the low-end of the graphite scale. Only after considerable experience are you likely to gain much benefit from the latest advances in graphite materials.

Graphite's main advantage over fiberglass in the eyes of most flycasters is its exceptional weight-to-power ratio. Flyrodders like it for other reasons too, among them outstanding recovery. This means, that, at the end of your casting strokes, the graphite rod straightens and becomes still much faster. To the eye, recovery looks virtually instantaneous with most graphite rods. Glass and bamboo tend to "wobble" considerably longer, and so transmit waves to the line that reduce casting efficiency.

Early graphite flyrods had detractors among those who prefer a rod with slow action, since all of them were very fast. But graphite now can be made into flyrods that suit anyone's taste in action.

In general, flyrods become heavier—in action, strength and balancing line size—as their lengths increase. The variations to this rule-of-thumb are relatively small until you reach 9 feet. all American flyfishermen shun rods longer than about 9 and a half feet, no matter how heavy the fishing. Therefore, you will find quite a large spread of actions in rods 9 to 9.5 feet long. Avid flycasters often own several rods of different actions in that size range—not only heavy ones for bass, salmon, saltwater and offshore, but also light ones for fishing lakes or wide streams.

Another rule-of-thumb in flyfishing is that when two rods use the same weight of line, the longer one will be easier to cast with, and capable of casting farther.

To elaborate on the terms "slow action" and "fast action" used earlier, they have nothing to do with line weight or balance. A "fast" rod is one in which most of the action is in the tip, with most of the shaft relatively stiff. A "slow" rod is one that distributes its bend over the entire length, with considerable flex all the way to the reel seat.

The beginning fly-fisherman will find a slow-action rod desirable because it is more forgiving of minor errors in timing.

It's possible to get a fair idea of the action of a glass rod by waving it around in the store. Not so with graphite rods. Most of them seem to be broomsticks—virtually actionless—when subjected to "store casting," and this is true of graphite spinning and baitcasting rods too.

FLYLINES

Flylines come in a wide variety of tapers and weights, the designated weight being that of the primary working portion of the line. For a beginner, it is of the utmost importance that the weight of the line be balanced to your rod's action for good casting performance. Fortunately, standardization in line labeling, plus the fact that all factory flyrods are labeled with recommended line sizes, makes this job pretty easy.

Standardized line labeling means that you don't have to remember actual line weight, in grams, but only relative weight, as defined by a standard numbering system. Although both smaller and larger line sizes are available, the common range of line weights runs from No. 4 (for light rods used for small trout or panfish) to No. 12 (balancing heavy rods used for tarpon or billfish).

In the standard labeling system, letters are used both before and after the weight number, and these denote the particular line's characteristics.

Letters in front of the number refer to the TAPER of the line—L stands for level; DT for double taper; WF for weight-forward taper. Letters behind the number refer to the BUOYANCY of the particular line: F for floating; S for sinking; I for intermediate or slow-sinking; FS for floating-sinking (only the tip sinks). There are also specialty lines, such as shooting heads, that wear additional prefixes or suffixes.

The LEVEL LINE, as the name denotes, has no taper at all.

Level

Double taper

Weight-forward
Flyline tapers

The DOUBLE TAPER LINE features identical thin tapers at both ends of a thick middle section. Designed for utmost delicacy in presenting small flies to trout, the double taper is seldom chosen for other kinds of fishing. Anglers who find the double taper suitable for their fishing needs also save money, because this line can be reversed—in effect giving them a brand-new line when their old one becomes tired and frazzled at the tip.

The WEIGHT-FORWARD LINE (sometimes called TORPEDO TAPER) has a short, thin tip section which swells abruptly to a thick portion, near the tip. This thick portion averages about 20 feet long. Behind it, the rest of the line is very thin and is referred to as the "running line." Weight-forward tapers are designed for long casting, particularly with heavy or bulky flies. Within the Weight-Forward family are such designations as "Bug taper," "Saltwater taper" and "Rocket taper." All are true weight-forwards, differing mainly in the length of the "torpedo" portion. Those with shorter heads can be put into action with a minimum of false casting. Especially useful for bass fishing and in salt water, these are the "bug" and "saltwater tapers."

The SHOOTING TAPER, in effect, is nothing more than the forward portion of a weight-forward line. The angler attaches this head to a very thin running line of his own choice. The running line may be of limp monofilament, braid, or simply a very, very thin flyline that is marketed as running line. Only after a flyfisherman becomes proficient with standard weight-forward lines is he likely to start looking at shooting tapers, which offer extra distance to the good caster.

We have seen that flylines come in different weights and different tapers. In addition, there are lines that float and lines that sink. The great majority of flylines have always been designed to float, but with today's emphasis on using fly tackle in virtually every angling situation imaginable, from shallow streams and flats to mighty rivers and deep channels, sinking lines are very popular. Even in waters where floating lines are the standard, sinking lines can often salvage some action on a day when the fish aren't rising.

Again, standard line labeling tells the buyer the three things he needs to know about a flyline—its weight, taper, whether it sinks or floats and, if a sinker, whether it sinks fast, slow or in between.

Only the number (not the letters) is important to rod balance. If a rod, for example, is suited to a No. 8 line, it can be used with any line that bears that number, regardless of taper and regardless of whether the line floats or sinks. Practiced casters can, by adjusting the amount of line they work with during the cast, do very well with line weights somewhat lower or higher than the basic weight for which the particular rod is designed. But beginners should stick to the recommendations.

Level lines are the least expensive, but the best for learning the basic mechanics and timing of flycasting. Moreover, level lines are functional enough for much freshwater and saltwater fishing—at least those kinds where great distance and delicate presentation are not of utmost importance.

All this means you can learn with a level line. You cannot take advantage of a weight-forward anyway, until after you master the mechanics and timing of flycasting. At that point you can put aside your inexpensive level line and get a weight-forward taper (of the same number, remember) in order to advance your blossoming skills.

FLYREELS AND BACKING LINE

Until you get into steelhead, salmon or saltwater fishing, your reel is the least important component of your fly outfit. It serves only to hold the line, so you might as well get the least expensive reel you can find, and the smallest one which will hold your line without crowding.

Most single-action reels are inexpensive. They are called single-action because they contain no gears; the spool revolves one turn for every turn of the crank.

Some people find automatic flyreels desirable for freshwater fishing. These have no crank at all. You wind up a spring mechanism and then retrieve line as needed by pressing a trigger with your finger. Automatic reels are not suitable when backing line must be used.

For saltwater flyfishing, as well as for salmon and steelhead, you'll be after fish that make long runs—possibly much longer than the length of your flyline, which is only around 90 feet. Now your reel becomes important because it has a part to play—like any other fishing reel—in fighting and bringing in the fish. The reel now must have a larger capacity in order to hold not only your flyline, but an attached quantity of backing line, which usually is of braided Dacron. It is also desirable to use a reel with an adjustable drag—and downright necessary if you go after real ocean toughies, such as tarpon and offshore fish. However, many of the smaller but

Single-action fly reel   Automatic fly reel

long-running saltwater fish (including bonefish) can safely be fought from a reel with merely a strong click mechanism rather than a sophisticated adjustable drag.

Many large-capacity flyreels are of the familiar single-action design with ventilated sideplates and the simple click-type drag referred to above. Although a few of these are rather costly, most are relatively inexpensive. The elite class of flyreels is that containing the solid, hand-machined beauties that provide utmost strength, smooth adjustable drag mechanisms and, of course, a helping of prestige. The cost of these runs into the hundreds of dollars, although there are quite a few makers these days and a reasonably wide spread of prices. Machined reels are pretty much necessary for the big saltwater species, such as tarpon and billfish, that are being chased by modern flyfishermen: however, many inshore and freshwater fishermen use them too.

In any event, you must choose a reel that will hold the flyline you intend to use, along with the amount of backing you prefer. For trout and salmon, a minimum of 100 yards of backing is desirable. For salt water, the minimum should be 200 yards inshore and 300 or more offshore. The biggest machined reels, designed for billfish and tuna, hold 500 to 600 yards of backing, depending on the diameter of the backing line chosen.

There are no rules regarding the test of backing line, but you should always use backing that is considerably stronger than the lightest section of your leader (see separate section on flyfishing leaders)—this to reduce the possibility of having the backing break first, causing you to lose the expensive flyline. There is much leeway, but 20-pound-test is a common backing size for salmon and inshore salt water; 30-pound test for tarpon and offshore fishing.

TOURNAMENT OR IGFA TACKLE

The International Game Fish Association (IGFA) keeps official world records in various line classes. Those classes have come to be accepted as handy labels to describe rods and reels that were designed for (or at least are very well suited for) fishing a particular size of line.

When someone refers to a "20-pound outfit," he is not talking about a set that weighs 20 pounds, but one that is scaled and balanced for fishing with 20-pound-class line.

Matched sets, and the quality rods and reels that make them up are referred to variously as "IGFA tackle," "Tournament tackle," or "class tackle." Tournament tackle includes some of the highest priced rods and reels in the industry and none of it is cheap. However, much of it is moderately priced and entirely adequate to the proposed tasks. For that matter, you should note that the IGFA does not require world-record catches to be made on fancy gear at all. That group does not care if you catch your record on a thousand-dollar matched outfit, or a bargain-basement combo, so long as your line tests within limits and your tackle meets specifications.

Still, the angler who intends to do a lot of offshore gamefishing should definitely invest in tournament tackle, for the simple reason that these matched outfits will do the best possible job in their particular line categories.

TOURNAMENT RODS

Rods designed for fishing in the various IGFA classes are offered by many manufacturers and custom builders and are plainly labeled as to class, so there is little confusion in picking out a rod of the right specifications. You can indeed shop for price, however.

IGFA class rods are frequently fitted with an entire set of roller

Traditional "tournament" rod

guides and a roller top, although a few have a roller first guide, roller top and ring guides in between. Obviously, those with all rollers cost more—and are worth more. IGFA rods also are characterized by a hard butt with a gimbal slot in the end. The slot, of course, is for fitting to the gimbal of a fishing chair or a gimbal belt.

Reel seats often are of strong and dependable chrome-on-brass construction. In light classes, graphite seats may be used. In the heaviest classes and most expensive rods, the seats are sometimes machined from solid barstock of special alloys.

The butts must be of strong material to resist scarring and gouging in metallic rodholders. Wood is the most common on less expensive rods. Solid fiberglass and fiberglass-graphite composites are used too, as are butts of heavy anodized aluminum tubing.

Most of the shafts (blanks) are of tubular fiberglass or graphite-glass composite material. Solid glass is often used too, and is very good indeed.

BIG-GAME REELS

The reels used in making up matched sets for line-class fishing are divided into two broad categories:

(1) Reels with a freespool lever and a separate star-drag mechanism. These reels generally are inexpensive but quite sturdy and dependable.

(2) Reels that incorporate the free-spool and drag-setting lever into a single unit. In full forward position, the lever gives maximum preset drag. When the lever is in full rearward position, the reel is in freespool. You have your choice of any drag in between the extremes at any time. The presetting of the drag range is handled by a separate adjusting device.

Obviously, the single-lever reel offers a dramatic advantage over star-drag models, which do not offer instant and positive drag

Star-drag ocean reel

changes—an advantage which is especially welcome when using heavier tests of line for big ocean fish, such as marlin and giant tuna. Different drag pressures are called for at different stages of a battle with a monster fish. With the single-lever, the angler can change drag settings at will, without risk of applying too much pressure at the wrong time and breaking the line.

All single-lever reels (also called dual-drag reels because of the presetting feature) are expensive, but some brands cost more than others. The price gap between single-lever and star-drag reels is not due as much to the sophisticated drag as it is to overall quality of material and workmanship. At the high end, spools are machined from solid bars of special-alloy aluminum, and more hand machine work may go into other parts as well.

Most reels today are labeled according to the size of line they best handle—for instance, 20, 50 or 130. Some labels suggest a range of appropriate sizes, as 50-80. In any case, the sizes are easy to sort out.

Dual-drag machined
ocean reel

However, some currently marketed ocean reels—both star-drag and single-lever—date back to the days when lines were classified by the number of threads they contained, rather than actual breaking strength. Those reels use a strange size-designation system made up of numbers and slashes and maybe fractions too. Examples: 2/0, 3/0, 4/0, 9/0 and 12/0.

The larger the number, the larger the reel. The number also gives at least a broad clue as to the appropriate size of line, although there is considerable latitude. For instance, you might use 20-pound line on a 2/0 or 3/0. You might use 30-pound line on either a 3/0 or 4/0. To continue, 50-pound line on a 6/0, 7.5/0 or 9/0; 80-pound on a 9/0 or 10/0; 130-pound on a 10/0, 12/0 or 14/0. Your final choice, of course, would depend on how much capacity you desire. It isn't a bad idea at all to spool up with considerably more line than you would normally think necessary. This is especially true when big-game fishing with heavier classes of line, but valid, too, in the lighter classes. You will be able to cut back line (for re-rigging, abrasion, etc.), and still be sure of having a usable amount for a long time.

In any event, offshore experts consider 400 yards as a minimum amount for the 12, 20 and 30-pound classes; 600 yards for heavier lines. In practice, most choose reels that will hold considerably more line than those suggested minimums.

STANDUP TACKLE

Not too long ago, the idea of fishing with heavy tackle for big-game species, without the aid of a fighting chair, would have been considered nonsensical.

Many offshore anglers did (and still do) prefer to stand while waging battles with billfish and other bluewater foes—but only when fishing the lighter IGFA line classes with their correspondingly light outfits. Most considered 30-pound as the heaviest tackle that was practical for "hand-holding," although a few he-men would

Matched standup tackle can subdue the largest gamefish.

occasionally stand and heave with 50-pound gear. Harnesses of any sort were seldom used while standing with light tackle. The light rods simply rested in belt-mounted gimbals.

As for the 80- and 130-pound classes—forget it. The common view was that it would take a wrestling champ just to hold the weight of such outfits while remaining erect, and at least a Superman to wage battle for prolonged periods while applying drag pressures ranging up to 40 pounds and sometimes even higher.

Actually that view was quite correct. It would indeed have required superhuman strength to perform such a task with standard big-game tackle and gimbal belts.

But that was before partyboats on the southern California coast (and later on the North Atlantic shore too) began taking anglers on long-range, multi-day trips in search of huge tuna weighing upwards of 100 pounds; occasionally several hundred pounds. The rails of partyboats are not lined with fighting chairs, and so specialized tackle had to be developed that would allow those adventurous anglers to use heavy lines and apply heavy drag while standing—and not suffer broken bones or hernias in the process.

The kind of gear we currently refer to as "standup tackle" evolved from that challenge, and it covers more than just rods and reels. Entirely new types of harnesses and belts had to be engineered to complete the system. Today a wide variety of all standup components is available. The harnesses and belts will be covered in the section on Accessories.

STANDUP RODS

Standup-style rods are now being marketed for not only the 50-, 80- and 130-pound IGFA classes but also for lighter work as well. Light-class standup rods simply give the offshore angler an alternative to the traditional "tournament" rods already discussed: however, in the heavy classes they are not merely an option but a downright necessity for all who want to stand on their own two feet and

Standup rod

catch a true big-game trophy.

Superficially similar to traditional tournament rods, the standup design can be immediately identified by two prominent features— a shorter butt and much longer foregrip. The overall length is also shorter and the blank is a fast-taper design—not the slow or parabolic action of most traditional offshore blanks. Most standup rods are 5.5 feet long, with 6 feet being as long as you're likely to see. By contrast, traditional trolling rods run 6.5 or 7 feet in length.

The short butt of an offshore rod will rest in the low-slung gimbal of a standup harness, enabling the angler to crank with his right arm in a comfortably low position—far less tiring than if he had to lift his arm to reach the crankhandle. At the same time, the long foregrip allows him to hang onto the rod with his left arm extended straight in front of him. Because of the harness, either or both hands can be removed from the tackle at any time to rest while the fish is running.

The combination of harness and belt is so situated as to allow the angler's lower back and legs to do most of the work in keeping up the pressure on a big fish. The rugged part of a struggle with a giant tuna or billfish is the effort to bring the fish close enough to gaff. Often as not, particularly with tuna, there is the task of heaving up a great weight from far below the surface, and this is where the standup system shines. What happens, basically, is that the opposing forces of the resisting fish and the well-harnessed angler combine to put a strong bend in the rod, which, being extra-powerful and of fast-taper design, then does much of the pumping automatically as it attempts to recover from the bend. Additional pumping is, of course, provided by the angler as he rocks backward and forward by leg power, keeping his back erect.

Other than sheer strength, there are no special requirements for reels used in standup fishing. They can be evaluated as already described for tournament reels.

BOAT TACKLE

Fishing gear designed primarily for still-fishing and trolling in salt water or big lakes is often referred to as "boat tackle." The term

Heavier tackle is needed to keep fish like this grouper out of the rocks.

34

implies gear that is not well suited to casting.

Technically, standup outfits and the matched sets of tournament tackle described earlier come under the heading of boat tackle: however, boat tackle is more commonly thought of as a workhorse sort of gear that can be pressed into adequate use for everything from bottom fishing to surface trolling.

Boat rod, plain butt

Boat rod, gimbal butt

BOAT RODS

Many boat rods are built around solid fiberglass blanks; many others of tubular glass. Graphite-glass composites are seen too. Solid fiberglass is the best choice for strength and durability combined with low price and so is pretty much standard on partyboats of the Atlantic Coast and Gulf of Mexico. Since casting action is of no importance at all, solid glass blanks are used even on some high-priced boat outfits. Although the great majority of boat rods are moderately priced, the cost can climb because of more and better guides and other hardware.

Boat rods can be found in lengths as short as five feet but the 6- or 6½-foot models will prove the most satisfactory for all-around saltwater use.

The most specialized of boat rods these days is the downrigger rod, used mostly for salmon and trout trolling in the Great Lakes and on the Pacific Coast, but also for king mackerel and other "downrigger" species along the Atlantic and Gulf shores. Downrigger rods are quite long—averaging 8 or 8.5 feet—and are whippy enough to take a pronounced bend when the bait is deployed and the fishing line is affixed to the underwater release device. In its ready, or bent, mode, the rod serves as a strike indicator; if it suddenly straightens up, it means that the line has been released—hopefully by a striking fish. The "forgiving" whippy action of a good downrigger rod also is desirable for fighting salmon and large trout, from which hooks are all-too-easily pulled if you apply too much pressure at the wrong time.

Your own choice of a boat rod must necessarily be based on the size line you plan to use. Most boat rods you'll find in tackle stores are best suited for lines ranging between 30- and 50-pound-test; however, there are plenty of light models available that handle 15- or 20-pound line, and some very heavy ones (often with a first roller guide and roller top) made for 80- or 100-pound line, or for wire line.

Outfits featuring 40-or-50-pound line fill the bill nicely as all-around rigs for the fellow who may go partyboat fishing for grouper or cod one day, then hang inshore and try for tarpon or striped bass the next. That rig might even get by for bluewater fishing once in a while.

Anglers who specialize would, of course, scale their boat tackle accordingly. They might choose 30-pound line if such species as king mackerel or big bluefish are primary targets; or 60-80-pound test if the specialty is bulldogging large bottom fish from sunken caverns.

Most of the aforementioned downrigger rods are designed for use with lines testing from 10 to 20 pounds.

BOAT REELS

Obviously, choosing a suitable reel for your boat rod also depends primarily on line size. As a rule, the reel should have a minimum capacity of 200 yards for lake, bay or most inshore fishing. Anyone who sometimes uses his boat tackle in offshore fishing, whether for pelagic species, bottom fish or a potluck effort at either, should pick a reel that holds at least 300 yards of his chosen line, and preferably 400.

All reels worthy of consideration, whether for light line or heavy, will have a free-spool lever and a star-drag adjustment device and a metal spool. The lower-priced ocean reels mentioned earlier in the IGFA category, make fine boat reels and should be the top choice for anglers who venture to blue water now and again, or who use heavy line in nearshore waters, but a variety of alternative reel choices can be found in various sizes and price categories.

Among the most popular these days are the level-wind models offered by several manufacturers. The level-wind mechanism is the very same as has long been found on baitcasting reels, and the big advantage, of course, is that it lays line on the spool evenly, so that

Boat reel

Level wind boat reel

the fisherman does not have to take pains to do this job manually. Line that piles up on one side of the spool during the heat of battle can prevent further retrieving of line and lead to lost fish.

No experienced saltwater angler trusts a level-wind reel to hold up to long-running or fast-running ocean heavyweights, but they are ideal for much inshore fishing—up to and including striped bass, bluefish, snook and tarpon—and for salmon trolling. Charterboat skippers, along with private-boat anglers who fish several rods at once, love the convenience of not having to make sure that novice anglers aboard their vessels keep the lines evenly wrapped.

Level-wind reels generally are spooled with light lines, ranging from 10 to perhaps 30 pounds, and they are frequently sold as combos with downrigger rods.

Monofilament line is by far the best all-around choice for a boat outfit, being less expensive, more "forgiving" and faster sinking than braided line. Therefore, it is important to make sure your reel does not have a plastic spool, which can be destroyed by pressures created by stretchy monofilament. If you have a reel with a plastic spool, use braided line. Plastic spool reels are cheapies and, fortunately, have just about disappeared from dealer shelves.

Refer to the section on IGFA tackle to get an idea of capacity with reels marked by the "O" system—3/0, 6/0, etc.

Many boat reels, however, aren't marked by a standard system at all, but only by a hodgepodge of trade names and arbitrary numbers. With those, the only way to determine capacity is to read the brochure.

SURF TACKLE

Surf comes in all degrees of wave action, from none to booming breakers. Depending on conditions, and on how far you have to heave your chosen baits or lures, you can use virtually any kind of casting tackle to fish the surf—down to and including flyrods and

Surf reel

light spinning outfits.

The term "surf tackle," however, is applied to rather stout, long-distance casting equipment—gear designed to toss lures or sinkers weighing several ounces far out over the breakers to reach distant holes or sloughs.

Conventional surf rods (spinning gear for surf fishing is discussed in the section on spinning tackle) are characterized by stout tips and very long butts. Overall length may range from as little as 8 feet to as much as 14, sometimes even longer.

The stoutest of all surf outfits are those used for tossing out bottom rigs with heavy pyramid sinkers—mainly in quest of huge red bass or black drum on the Atlantic Coast. It takes a lot of rod to handle five or six ounces of sinker, and so the tips of these heavy-duty sticks are as big around as your thumb.

Though longer rods are available, many surf specialists agree that 10 or 11 feet is the best all-around length range.

Surf reels are similar in design to other free-spool, star drag salt-water reels, but they generally have a wider spool and other features designed to improve casting efficiency. They may be called

Level wind surf reel

"squidding reels" or "saltwater casting reels," as well as "surf reels." Among the best for surf-fishing with lines in the 12-20-pound range—especially monofilament lines—are the oversize versions of some popular baitcasting reels.

Bigwater surf anglers, however, tend to favor heavier lines and are apt to choose "squidding line" over monofilament. Squidding line is of braided nylon, in tests ranging from 18 to 54 pounds. The most popular sizes are 27 and 36 pounds. The odd pound-test designations are holdovers from the days of linen line.

Surfing specialists will own at least two outfits and, like all other anglers, probably will have more than that. One would be one of the "broomstick" rods described earlier, used with 36-pound line for heaving out heavy bottom rigs or his biggest metal squids. The other would be lighter—a more flexible and perhaps longer rod, which he uses with lighter line to throw bass plugs and other popular lures, plus bottom rigs with sinkers weighing two or three ounces.

That second outfit might be a conventional surf rig with 18- or 27-pound squidding line, or it might be a surf-spinning outfit with 20 or 25-pound monofilament.

Stout gear like this is perfect for targeting big fish from shore.

Chapter 2

Baits Rigs & Tackle

Specialty Rigs and Poles

KITE FISHING SETUP

A fishing kite is used to present live baits well away from an anchored or drifting boat—or even from shore, provided the wind is in a favorable direction. The kite can also be used in the manner of an outrigger to troll artificial or rigged baits.

Don't try to build your own kite; buy a manufactured one.

The first illustration shows the arrangement of kite, kite line and fishing lines in a typical deployment from a small boat. The kite can be flown either from a manufactured, single-action kite reel with integral rod, or from a large fishing reel with heavy fishing rod. In either case, the kite line should test at least 50 pounds. On a hand reel, braided line should be used. Either braided or monofilament line will work when using a converted fishing reel as a kite reel.

Two line-release pins are attached to the kite line. The most popular type—the Black—is illustrated and widely sold. Complete kite reels, ready to fish with line and pins in place, are available.

If you rig your own kite reel, note that the release pins run freely on the kite line, and that one pin must have larger line holes than the other. These pins are sometimes sold in pairs, each with holes of a different size, but if you have two pins with the same size holes, you must enlarge the holes on one of them with an electric drill. You will also need two barrel swivels of different sizes. One swivel, perhaps a No. 7, must be large enough to stop the pin that has the smaller holes, yet small enough to allow the pin with the larger holes to run past it. The other swivel, say a No. 5 or 3, must be large enough to stop the pin with the larger holes.

Proceed as follows:

1. Tie an offshore snapswivel to the end of the kite line. This will be your attachment for the kite.

2. About 50 feet back from that snapswivel, cut the line and slide on the release pin that has the smaller holes, making sure that the release arm of the pin will open downward. Next, tie on the small-

er swivel. Stopped by the swivel, your first pin will slide no farther down the line, but is free (upon retrieving the line) to travel upward, all the way to the kite connection.

3. About 40 or 50 feet from the first swivel, cut the line again. Now slide the release pin with the larger hole onto the line and tie the larger swivel below it. Last, tie the kite line to the other eye of the larger swivel and your rigging is complete.

4. As your kite goes up, the first release pin will stop at the small swivel. Lock or hold the kite reel and place one fishing line in that pin.

5. Slowly let out more kite line, while the angler lets out his fishing line. When the second release pin stops at the larger swivel, lock the kite reel once more and attach the second fishing line to the second pin.

6. Finally, by simultaneously letting out kite line and fishing line—and by alertly handling the fishing reels to adjust the position of the baits up or down as necessary—you get both baits the desired distance from the boat. Now lock the kite reel and you are in business. You must continually monitor the baits, however, to take up or let out line as the need arises.

When you crank in the kite line to replace baits or end the trip, the lower release pin will run up the line, "jump" the small swivel and finally come to rest beside the upper pin at the kite-connecting snapswivel. This makes for easy handling and storing.

OUTRIGGERS

For trolling rigged baits at, or just under, the surface, outriggers are a tremendous aid. They are long poles that angle outward from each side of the boat, thus allowing the fishermen to troll more lines. They also provide a small amount of "dropback," or slack, after a striking fish snaps the line from the outrigger pin. This

43

makes it easier to hook sailfish and certain other species. Outriggers are standard equipment on offshore sportfishing boats, and can easily be mounted on smaller boats as well, using components available at marine stores in coastal areas—a gunnel mount that holds a long pole, usually of tubular aluminum. Ordinarily, the mount is a two-position one that allows the pole to stand upright when running. Or the poles can be removed from the mounts and placed on the deck (or left ashore when they won't be needed.)

The outrigger line is usually of very heavy monofilament, 200-pound-test or more. Connected at the ends by means of crimped sleeves, the circle of line runs through guides on the pole, and trough a large glass eye that is connected via a shock cord to a cleat forward of the mount, as illustrated. Thus rigged, the line remains taut and can be lowered and raised by hand and left in any position desired. A release clip of some sort—various kinds are available, including ordinary clothespins—is incorporated into the outrigger line, also by using crimped sleeves. More than one clip may be used on each outrigger.

You take your fishing line at the rodtip and clip it to the outrigger pin. Then you simultaneously feed line from the fishing reel while hoisting the outrigger line. With a little practice, and a reel that has a clicker mechanism to prevent backlashing, one person can easily do the job.

The clip shown in the detail is he Black Clip, identical to that used with a fishing kite.

DOWNRIGGERS

By far the most efficient tool ever designed for deep trolling is the

Wheel

Crank

End view of Downrigger

Manual downrigger reel

Rod tip

Rod holder

Downrigger

Trolling direction

Fishing line

Flasher or Dodger

Lure

Mounting bracket

Wire line

Quick-release mechanism

Torpedo

Downrigger setup

Trolling direction

Trolling line

Rod line

Black line period

Trolling weight

Lure

Increases this distance

Increases drop back time

Trolling direction

Trolling line

Rod line

Trolling weight

Teaser

downrigger. It is the only deep-fishing device that allows the angler to present his baits or lures at selected and variable depths, and to keep them there.

Homemade versions of the downrigger were in scattered use for many years, but not until after the introduction of salmon into the Great Lakes in the 1960s did downrigger fishing become a standard angling system. Now, manufactured downriggers and accessories have reached a high level of dependability, portability and sophistication.

Great Lakes anglers seeking various species of salmon and large trout remain the chief users of downriggers, but the system expanded rapidly to other waters and downriggers are now commonly used in saltwater fishing on all coasts.

Coho and chinook salmon can be caught near the surface in spring and fall but throughout the summer can only be taken deep. Coho prefer a temperature of about 53 degrees Fahrenheit, and this may at times be 200 feet down.

But even at much shallower levels, whether for salmon or saltwater battlers, the downrigger still excels as a fishing tool, simply because it will work at any level you desire.

Downriggers are large reels spooled with wire cable. To the end of the cable is fitted a heavy weight, which is lowered via an arm-and pulley arrangement. On or near the weight is a release device to which the fishing line is clipped.

The weight carries the line and lure to the desired depth, whereupon the downrigger is locked. A counter connected to the spool tells you how much line is out. A little bit of trial-and-error is still involved, however, because the cable—no matter how heavy the weight, will not stay straight down as the boat moves. In practice, you will have to let out perhaps twice as much cable as the desired depth in order to reach that level; the exact difference depends on boat speed, size and design of the trolling weight, and sea conditions. A good depthfinder—especially one with side-scanning capability—is considered not just an aid to productive downrigger fishing but a virtual necessity.

Several designs of downrigger weights are available, the most common shapes being ball and torpedo. Trolling planers (see next heading) are used by some anglers on their downriggers to replace the traditional heavy weights. Their users think they are more efficient at attaining—and maintaining—selected depths with less bellying of the cable.

Once a fish is hooked, the downrigger weight should be cranked up out of the way. Motorized downriggers make this job easier, but hand-cranking is not too exhausting a task—thanks to the wide diameter of the reel—and many saltwater anglers prefer manual downriggers because of their dependability under corrosive conditions.

Two downriggers, one on each corner of the transom, is a com-

Downriggers add a new dimension to trolling.

mon installation. Great Lakes charter skippers and other routine users of downriggers often mount several on their boats. They may place additional units on the gunnels, with arms positioned outward, or modify the transom to accept downrigger mounts at several positions.

Once a mounting bracket is installed, its downrigger can be set up and removed at will.

THE TROLLING PLANER

Diving planers—traditionally rigged directly to the fishing line—are less expensive devices than downriggers but they do a good job of allowing anglers to troll baits at depths that are difficult to achieve, if not impossible, with heavy sinkers, or even wire lines.

Planers are weighted, but the lead has little to do with depth potential. It serves only to keep the planer in the proper attitude, which is such that water pressure on the sloped face of the planer forces the device downward. It's the same principle that causes big-lipped artificial lures to dig deep when they are trolled or retrieved rapidly.

Several sizes of planer are offered. Planer size, combined with trolling speed, how much line is out, line diameter and weight of lure and terminal tackle, all affect the running depth of the lure. Even more than with downriggers, much experimenting will be needed to determine individual needs and desires. Again, a depth-sounder is a great help.

The design of manufactured planers allows them to "trip" after a fish is hooked. The running attitude is thereby changed, eliminating the water pressure so that the angler can fight his fish, even on fairly light tackle, without much extra strain. Note, however, that considerable strain is exerted on the rod while the planer is being trolled, so fairly stout rods are necessary.

Rigging is easy. Tie your main fishing line to the front eye of the planer (the one nearest the lead sinker), and your leader—or, if using no leader, a few extra feet of line—to the rear eye. Your lure, of course, will go at the end of that shorter line. If using wire leader, rig the planer in about the first one-third of the wire.

"POOR MAN'S DOWNRIGGER"

A planer can be made into a "poor man's downrigger" by the simple expedient of tying a separate line to its front eye and attaching

Planers are a simple, economical way to troll baits deep.

47

a release clip to the rear eye. The fishing line is attached to this clip and paid out as the planer is lowered on its separate line. When a fish strikes, the fishing line snaps free and the planer can be hauled aboard while the angler fights his fish with no encumbrance at all. Various outrigger and downrigger clips will do this job well.

This arrangement does not even approach a true downrigger in efficiency or versatility, but it is cost-effective and can serve the needs of many trollers very well—particularly those who generally do their trolling at one or two established depths. After experimenting to determine the amount of line needed to reach the selected depths, the angler can attach just the needed length of planer line to a stern cleat. Heavy braided line is a good choice because it handles easily. An alternative idea is to rig the separate planer to the line of a heavy rod and reel. This may make retrieving the planer a bit easier.

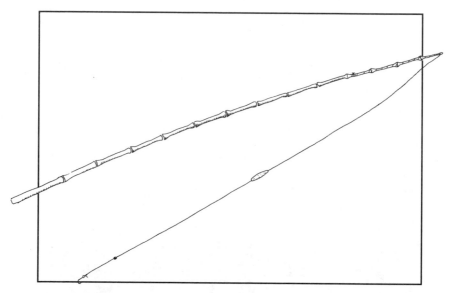

RIGGING THE CANEPOLE

Canepoles are not only maintaining their popularity, but are actually increasing in use as the years go by. Kids use them, of course, but so do countless grownups. Nobody can dispute the effectiveness of a pole for producing good strings of bream, perch, catfish and many other species.

Plenty of bass and trout are caught on canepoles too—sometimes by chance, but often by design.

Advances in poles have managed to keep pretty well abreast of advances in rods and reels. You can still buy the traditional bamboo pole just about everywhere, and in a great variety of lengths and actions. You can also buy jointed bamboo poles in

48

two, three or four pieces.

And heading the array of poles are the modern, telescoping fiberglass sticks, which cost a few bucks but which stow and transport more easily and generally outlast far more than their equivalent cost in canepoles.

As a rule of thumb, you should use as long a pole as you can comfortably handle—although, of course, shorter poles better fit certain requirements, such as fishing small, bush-line creeks. Most fishermen in open water use 12- or 14-footers; a few prefer 16, or even 18, feet of pole in their hands.

For panfishing—where the pole really shines—the line should be of monofilament averaging 10 to 15 pounds in test. Some prefer lighter line, but panfish are not too selective, and the extra test will save a lot of rerigging.

First, tie the line snugly around the pole about two feet down from the tip—just under the third or fourth "knuckle" of the bamboo. Then spiral the line upward and tie it around the tip. A good way to do this is to half-hitch it several times and then tape the end. Should the tip break, you're protected by the second tie and may not lose your fish or rig. Glass poles generally feature an eye at the end to make tying easy.

Your line should be about the same length as the pole—not much longer or it will become difficult to handle; not much shorter or it will limit your reach and/or fishing depth. By taping a small cleat near the butt of the pole, you can keep extra line on hand to be paid out when needed. Conversely, if your line happens to be too long, you can wrap the excess around the cleat. A rubber band or tape is used to keep line snug on the cleat. Small and inexpensive canepole reels serve the same purpose.

Although the great majority of pole-fishermen use floats to signal a bite, some of the very best ones use no cork at all. They can better explore various depths, and are always sure of getting their bait to bottom when they want to, without having to test and adjust corks. It is surprisingly easy to feel a bite—even a nibble—with a pole. The movement of line through the water also signals a bite.

THE JIGGER POLE

"Jigger fishing" is probably the oldest known method of taking bass on an artificial lure—and is still one of the best. It doesn't appeal to every angler, and it would not qualify in bass tournaments, but it has always had a staunch, if small, corps of followers. Anyone who develops a knack for jigger fishing can produce bass like magic, particularly at night.

The system, also referred to as "skittering," "doodle-socking," and various other colloquial terms, was described by naturalist William Bartram in his writings on Florida during the period 1773-1778—and apparently it was long established even then.

A very strong pole is needed, 12 or 14 feet long, or even longer if the fisherman is strong enough to handle it. The line—only a couple of feet long—should test at least 40 pounds, but can be of either

49

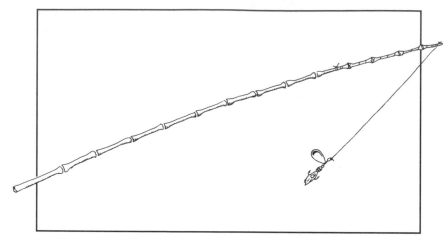

braid or monofilament. Tie it two or three joints back from the pole's tip, then spiral it to the tip and tie it again.

The jigger lure is often homemade, although a hefty spinnerbait, plastic eel or lizard, or a big weedless spoon with a plastic or pork trailer all work well. "Custom" lures incorporate several of those same elements, but commonly feature a large treble hook, dressed with feathers or hair, and a big spinner blade or propeller blade.

Far more important than design is the noise and splash the lure makes when manipulated on the surface.

The system is usually practiced by two people—one sitting in the bow of a boat and skittering the lure steadily, ahead of the boat and around snags or vegetation; the other in the stern, paddling or steering an electric motor. You can also jigger-fish by walking along shore, or wading.

When the bass hits, you don't lift the pole as you would when fishing for bream. You first jerk the pole toward you to set the hook, and then continue to handline the pole until the fish comes within reach of hand or net.

Unsporting, say some people. But nobody can deny that it not only is productive but often heart-stopping in its excitement.

CALCUTTA POLE

Sportsmen tend to sneer at the Calcutta pole as a "meat fisherman's" device. So it may be, but the fact remains that a lot of specialists use it for such heavy-duty jobs as catching snook from bridges or hauling jewfish from their lairs under mangrove banks or around pilings and other obstructions. The whole idea is to use something stout enough so you can simply overpower big fish—provided you have the necessary courage and muscle—in situations where rod-and-reel fishing normally is doomed to failure.

Use heavy braided line (130-pound-test or heavier) for attaching to the pole. Tie the line tightly around the pole three or four joints

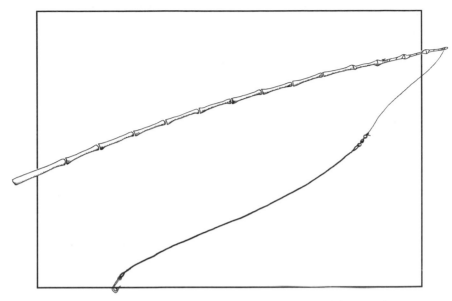

back from the tip, then spiral the line around the pole several times until you reach the top. Take two or three wraps around the tip, then half-hitch it several times. Wrap the tip tightly with strong tape. You should have a foot or two of line dangling from the tip, and to this you tie a heavy-duty swivel.

The rest of the line is made up of stout leader wire, at least No. 9. The overall length should be about the length of the pole.

Wrap the wire to both swivel and hook with the Haywire Twist. Only heavy-duty forged hooks should be used with this rig, or the hook is apt to straighten under the heavy pressure expected.

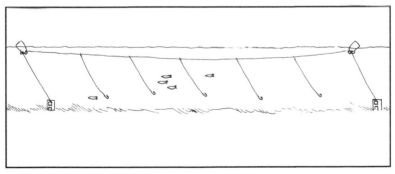

THE TROTLINE

Used mostly for catfish, the trotline is merely a long, stout line that has dropper lines coming off it at regularly spaced intervals. Each dropper line is fitted with a hook and, usually, a sinker. To

51

avoid the costs of sinkers, a trotliner may weight his droppers with old nuts or other scrap metal.

Many different baits can be used. Cut bait is a popular one. The bait doesn't necessarily have to rest on bottom, since trotlines are left out overnight, or longer, and catfish roam and feed throughout the water column after dark.

Ready made trotlines are available, usually with up to about 30 dropper lines and hooks. Commercial fishermen use much longer lines with many more droppers.

In areas where boat traffic is little problem, trotlines are often rigged as in the illustration—with buoys and heavy weights at either end. Sometimes the trotline is tied between two trees or snags. Or one end of the line can be tied to a tree on shore, and the other end anchored out in the water.

Be sure to check for legal restrictions on trotlines in your state, or in the local waters you plan to fish. They are sometimes prohibited, and sometimes limited as to length or number of hooks. Live bait is not allowed on trotlines in many jurisdictions.

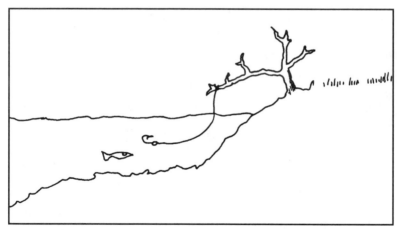

THE BUSH LINE

A pet of catfishermen is the bush line. These lines are normally tied to a number of springy branches along the bank of a river or creek before dark, then checked once or twice during the night, or next morning. The individual sets are short lengths of braided line with hooks tied to the end, baited with cutbait, liver, or the fisherman's secret potion. The line need only reach a foot or less under the surface. At night, catfish forage boldly and readily come to the top. When a fish is hooked, the springy limb "plays" it and keeps the line from breaking or the hook from pulling out.

As with trotlines, be sure to check the legality of bush lines in particular areas. Also be sure to remove all lines, along with any markers you might put out, the next day.

Simple tackle, rigged right, yields trophy results.

Chapter 3

Baits Rigs & Tackle

Fishing Lines and Terminal Tackle

Fishing Lines

Modern fishing lines are made of synthetic materials—mainly nylon monofilament, braided nylon and braided Dacron. They represent a great improvement over previously-used natural materials, such as cotton, silk and linen. The synthetics don't rot. They need not be dried after each use, and they are generally more uniform in strength and diameter.

BRAIDED NYLON lines are used mostly in certain kinds of casting. Many freshwater plug-casters prefer them, and they are the standard for surf-casting with conventional reels. Braid is softer and "limper" than monofilament, and spools better on revolving reels. It is less likely to kink or backlash than is monofilament. But, on the other hand, mono is thinner than braided nylon and allows more line to be used on the reel, and is also less visible in the water.

BRAIDED DACRON is used primarily as a saltwater trolling line. For this purpose, it is chosen over braided nylon because it is thinner and has very little stretch.

ULTRA-THIN BRAIDS, introduced in the early 1990s, comprise the newest family of fishing lines and are characterized by strength-to-diameter ratios that seem nearly incredible when compared to any other lines ever used for sportfishing. On average, these lines test as strong as monofilament lines three times as thick. They are built of many tiny strands of modern synthetic fibers, mostly polyethylene or Kevlar.

Although conceived as saltwater lines and offered mostly in the heavier tests, these new-generation lines also are available in light-tackle sizes and make outstanding choices for bass fishermen and others who do a great deal of casting, since their smaller diameters allow *both* greater casting distance *and* extra strength. With older kinds of line, a compromise would have to be made, with one of those features favored over the other. The thin braids also, of course, greatly extend the line-capacity of any reel on which they are spooled. Their chief disadvantage at this writing is high cost. Although the price figures to decline as competition increases, manufacturing costs alone will probably always keep them at a much more expensive level than monofilament.

MONOFILAMENT is the true all-purpose line for modern fishing. It should be used with *all* spinning reels, regardless of reel size, because the "springiness" inherent in even the limpest monofilaments helps increase casting performance with fixed-spool tackle. Mono is also widely used for plug-casting, for ocean trolling, and for saltwater fishing in general. And, of course, monofilament is used for leader material as well as for line.

The choice between braided Dacron line and monofilament for offshore trolling is largely a matter of personal preference. In IGFA line classes up through 50-pound, either type can be used, but Dacron is far less "stretchy" than monofilament. It takes an experienced hand to use the light classes of Dacron under conditions of maximum drag pressure and avoid breaking the line. Therefore, it is generally only the expert blue water angler who chooses Dacron over monofilament in the light and medium classes.

With 80- and 130-pound-class line (possibly even 50), the outlook is different. You're using heavy tackle and strong drag pressure, and the stretchy monofilament line tends to punish the angler too much physically. Besides, the soft Dacron spools and handles far better on the reel when using the thick 80- and 130-pound lines. For these reasons, Dacron has traditionally been chosen by heavy-tackle anglers who seek marlin and giant tuna.

The ultra-thin braids now give the offshore angler an extra choice—and one he will have to think over very carefully. On large reels, the thin stuff could prove to be a disadvantage, not only in cost but in tendency to "cut into" itself on the spool because of its smaller diameter. Both tendencies could be minimized by filling most of the spool with thicker line—Dacron or mono—and then "topping off" with a fighting length of the thin stuff.

Getting back to monofilament, the most widespread application for 80- and 100-pound-test mono is not for marlin and tuna, but for fishing for shark, big grouper, and other big but not overly active fish—especially when fishing very deep. Mono sinks far faster than Dacron. And you don't worry about the additional burden it imposes on you physically, because that sort of deep fishing requires a strong back no matter how you go about it. The ultra-thin braids would be a good choice here for individuals—but not for party and charter skippers who have to buy a lot of line.

CHOOSING MONOFILAMENT

There are many different brands of monofilament line, and they vary widely in handling qualities. There is really no "best" brand, or type, for all kinds of fishing. And price is not always a reliable guide to the best choice for your own fishing.

As a rule, the highest-priced lines are those which have been highly processed for limpness, and for the smallest ratio of breaking test to line diameter.

The limpest lines, of course, are a joy to handle because they lie on the spool beautifully and do not tend to bulge or spring off in unwanted fashion (it bears repeating that even the limpest monos, however, are not nearly so relaxed as braided lines, and that some spring is beneficial to spincasters).

For most freshwater fishing, limp lines are much to be preferred.

The saltwater angler, however, soon finds that the ultra-soft monofilaments are not his cup of tea. They may "fatigue" or weaken faster under the pressures of big fish, big lures and various other rigors of salty fishing. Also, the knot strength of some is below acceptable standards for ocean heavyweights.

Therefore, the saltwater man is quite willing to sacrifice some limpness for lines which better resist abrasion and "fatigue," and which—because they probably also have a slightly harder finish—provide greater knot strength.

Most of the major manufacturers now offer several different kinds (not grades) of monofilament lines so that anglers can pick out those that best fit the needs of various angling specialties.

HERE'S AN IMPORTANT WORD about line-test: In most cases, the line you buy will actually test heavier than is stated on the label. This is the way most anglers like it. But if you go in for competitive fishing in clubs and public tournaments, or if you have your aim set on possible world records, you want to make sure that your line *does not test heavier* than the allowable limit.

57

No matter what you may think of the metric system, the first impact of metric conversion in the world of sportfishing was a definite boon to American anglers, for it had the effect of giving their lines a safety margin of about 10 percent in the light-tackle classes when tested for world-record catches. The International Game Fish Association, keeper of world records, adopted the metric system for its line-test classes in 1976—not because it was trying to hasten American exposure to the metric system, but simply because the kilogram is the standard measurement of weight in most other countries. The IGFA, after all, keeps records worldwide.

Here's how the IGFA now lists its line classes for world records, and the maximum test in each class:

TABLE OF POUND-KILO MAXIMUMS

Pound-Class	Kilogram-class	Max. Test in Pounds
2	1	2.20
4	2	4.40
6	3	6.60
8	4	8.81
12	6	13.22
16	8	17.63
20	10	22.04
30	15	33.06
50	24	52.91
80	37	81.57
130	60	132.27

Since line classes now are listed by both pound-test and kilogram-test, and since the maximum allowable line strength is based on the kilogram class, it amounts to a liberalization for lines labeled in pounds. Before we bog down in decimal points, let's just say that many premium brands of line you buy nowadays will probably test in their labeled class, whereas, before liberalization, record-size catches made on standard lines often were thrown out because the line overtested. To play it safe, anglers had to pre-test their lines, or else buy special tournament-grade line. Of course, if record-chasing is your cup of tea, that's still a good idea.

That kind of fiddling with line-test always has been a headache for the record-seeking angler. And even though most fishermen don't actively seek records, they have frequently run afoul of line-test problems when they happened to catch one.

Avid light-tackle anglers recognized and welcomed the liberalized maximum tests, but failed to take into account the fact that in all cases, the tests listed are wet tests. The IGFA soaks lines before testing—and wet lines lose about 15 percent of strength. Therefore, anglers who continue to use "tournament" lines are short-changing themselves. They could be using line considerably stronger, yet still safely within allowable limits.

Perhaps the table below will clarify the point.

For comparison, let's look at "tournament" 12-pound line, as opposed to "regular" 12-pound line in the following table of light-line classes. Often, 12-pound tournament line will dry-test around 10 pounds. Take away 15 percent for wet-test, and the actual strength of the line is 8.5—nearly five pounds lighter than is allowed! Since you pay a premium price for "tournament" line, you might be dishing out extra money to buy yourself a substantial handicap.

TABLE OF WET AND DRY TESTS

Standard Label (Pounds)	Actual Dry Test Can Be	Wet Test Would Be	Allowable Wet Test Is
2	2.5	2.13	2.2
4	5	4.25	4.4
6	7	6.4.	6.6
8	10	8.5.	8.8
12	15	12.75	13.22
16	20	17	17.6
20	25	21.3	22
30	38	32.3	33

SPOOLING LINE

No matter what kind of line or what kind of reel you're using, it should be put on the spool under enough pressure to assure that it will not "dig in" to itself. Snug spooling on a spinning reel also helps assure that extra line will not spring off during the cast, and that one or more loops will not spring off simultaneously, thus causing a tangle. On a baitcasting reel, or revolving reel of any kind, loosely-spooled line often causes backlashes.

TO INSTALL LINE ON A REVOLVING SPOOL REEL, mount the reel firmly on the rod butt. Have someone hold the spool of line on a pencil or similar object to serve as an axle. Grasp the foregrip

of the rod with your left hand, and with the same hand extend your thumb and one or two fingers upward so that you can grasp the line simultaneously. As you crank the reel with your right hand, apply pressure to the line with the fingers of your left hand. You will have to judge the proper amount of pressure; very little is needed for light lines, but with lines of 50-pound or up, you will have to bear down hard and perhaps even wear a glove.

TO INSTALL LINE ON A SPINNING REEL, mount the reel firmly on the rod butt. Grasp the rod ahead of the foregrip with your non-cranking hand, and take the line in the same grasp, so that it runs between thumb and one or two fingers. Place your spool

of line on the floor. You do not allow the spool to revolve, but merely let the line slip off the end of it. Turn the reel crank as you apply light pressure with thumb and finger to the oncoming line. Use just enough pressure to assure a snug wrap.

Before spooling line in the manner described above, you must check the bail of your reel to see in which direction it travels around your reel spool. Bails on most spinning reels travel in a clockwise direction, therefore the line must slip off the supply spool in a counter-clockwise direction. Otherwise, severe twist will result. If line is coming off the supply spool in the wrong direction, you have only to turn the spool of line over and let it rest on the opposite end of the spool in order to change the unwrapping direction from clockwise to counterclockwise.

Hooks

Choosing a suitable hook for a particular type of fishing is really not such a confusing task as the inexperienced angler might believe. True, the angler is faced with a seemingly endless variation of pattern, finish and size—but he doesn't need a computer in order to make his choices, only a bit of common sense.

First, rid yourself entirely of the notion that an exact size of an exact pattern is necessary for fishing success. Certain patterns are desirable for different specialties, and you have to be somewhere in the neighborhood when it comes to size. But there is a great deal of leeway, as evidenced by the fact that even professional guides may have vastly different ideas as to what makes the best hook for a specific task. This discussion therefore, will not be overly concerned about trying to sort out subtle differences in the many named patterns on the market, but will stress general characteristics so that the angler will have a guideline for making his own choices.

HOOK SIZES

It helps to understand how hook sizes are designated.

Small hooks are scaled by a system of straight numbers—the larger the number, the smaller the hook. The biggest hook which is labeled by this system is a No. 1. Some very tiny hooks, used mostly for certain demanding types of trout fishing, might wear numbers as high as 20 or 22.

For some strange reason, hooks larger than No. 1 (as almost all saltwater and many freshwater hooks are) wear numbers that begin with No. 1/0, and go up as the hook size goes up. The largest sizes you're ever apt to see in gamefishing run from 14/0 to 20/0.

As already mentioned, you need not trouble yourself over determining an exact size. Usually, the effective range for a specific application spans several sizes. But there are two general considerations that must be taken into account.

First, the size of the hook is more often determined by the size of the bait than by the size of the fish you're after. This is particularly true of rigged saltwater baits, but valid in almost any baiting situation. You need a hook which will leave ample point and barb exposure after your bait is fixed to it. On the other hand, you don't want a hook so large that the live bait you're using is unable to swim naturally while carrying it; or so large that it throws a rigged bait out of balance and deprives it of attractive action.

Second, your hook must be strong enough to prevent its straightening out under the drag pressure you plan on using. This factor is not so critical in freshwater and light saltwater fishing with spinning tackle, as it is when you use heavy tackle. Still, it must be considered. Hook strength is increased slightly as size of the hook is increased—but only slightly. In marginal cases you can increase the size of your hook by a couple of numbers and feel safer. But to obtain any drastic change in strength, while keeping the size range within reasonable limits, you'll have to go to a different hook altogether—one of similar size but heavier, sturdier construction.

For anyone using light tackle (all kinds of casting gear, plus ocean tackle with lines up to 30-pound-test) here's a pretty good rule of thumb: When in doubt about choosing from among several available hooks in a range of no more than three size numbers, pick the smallest size. It is a much more common mistake to use a hook which is too large than one which is too small.

Style No. 84 — standard length, actual size

Following are some other hook characteristics which can help you make a common-sense choice.

FRESHWATER HOOKS

Hooks used in fresh water are generally made of lighter wire than hooks designed principally for use in the salt. The usual finishes are bronze and blue. Most fishermen feel a subdued tone is less likely to alert a potential biter, especially when using insect baits or bottom baits. Some live-baiters, however, do prefer a nickel plated or gold-plated hook.

Wading through the numerous patterns of freshwater hooks, we will consider only two basic designs. (1) The straight design, where the shank, the bend and the point are in a single plane: that is, if you lay the straight hook flat on a table, the point does not protrude, but lies as flat as the shank. (2) The offset hook, in which the point is bent to one side or other of the shank.

You can compare these two basic designs as follows: Place both hooks flat on a table, then place the palm of your hand over them, and also resting flat. Leave the eyes of both hooks free, outside your hand. Now (gently, of course) try to slide both hooks out from under your hand by pulling on the hook-eyes. The straight hook will slide out. The offset hook will either prick your hand or dig into the table surface (depending on the direction of the offset). You cannot slide it out.

Thus the offset hook is the choice of many fishermen, because it is less likely to be pulled from a fish's mouth without digging in.

On the other hand, the straight design will usually hook a striking fish, although occasionally it might miss one which an offset would have hooked. The difference in hooking percentage is slight, at best, but enough to swing many folks on the side of the offset.

Offset hooks, however, are not often used on artificial lures because they can affect lure balance and action.

Salmon egg hooks (Mustad 79791) above, and Aberdeen (Mustad 3261), right.

Sproat hooks (Mustad 3367), right, are standards for artificial worms. Special worm-hook models are the three at left.

There are numerous style variations, which you can find on hooks of either of the two basic designs—long shanks and short shanks, turned-up eyes and turned-down eyes, straight points and curved points.

Hooks with turned-up or turned-down eyes are used mainly in making certain artificial lures (flies and jigs, mostly). They are of little concern to the bait fisherman, except in a few specialties, such as fishing salmon eggs for trout. Hooks with turned down eyes also are used to make snells.

A long-shank hook is more easily removed from a fish after you catch him, and is often chosen by anglers for just that advantage. But hooks of normal and short-shank design are less likely to be noticed by fish, and so you may have to abandon the long-shank if it seems to be cutting down on your number of bites.

Some freshwater fishermen like to use panfish hooks made of very light wire that bends easily. When you get snagged on bottom, extra pressure straightens the hook and allows it to come free. You simply bend the light wire back into proper position and go on fishing. Naturally, you don't want the hook so light that it might bend when you have a fish on. And if you think you might hook a bass or big catfish while fishing for bream, then you definitely should use a hook of stouter wire.

SALTWATER HOOKS

If you haven't already done so, read the discussion on freshwater hooks for a comparison of the straight design and offset design, and for notes on point and eye variations.

In general, offset hooks make excellent choices for still-fishing in salt water with any sort of natural bait, live or dead. Straight design hooks may be freely substituted for offset hooks in any kind of still-fishing. However, the offset hooks probably have a slightly higher percentage of solid hookups.

Offset hook (Mustad 92673), above, and O'Shaughnessy (Mustad 3407).

Straight-design hooks should be used with all rigged saltwater baits (strip ballyhoo, mullet, etc.), because offset hooks sometimes impair trolling action.

Hooks with ringed eyes are used for most inshore fishing, and much offshore fishing as well (with fairly light tackle and reason-

Short-shank live bait hook (Mustad 94151)

Siwash or salmon hooks (Mustad 95160)

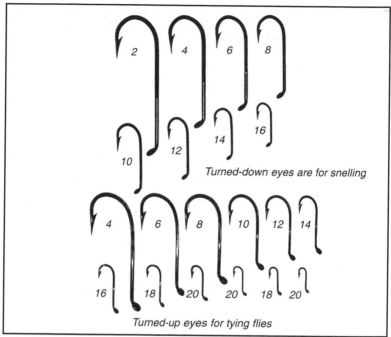

Turned-down eyes are for snelling

Turned-up eyes for tying flies

ably low drag).

Hooks with needle eyes (that is, with the eye drilled through the shank, rather than formed by bending the shank into a circle) are chosen by many offshore fishermen for blue water trolling and deep bottom fishing, particularly with heavier tackle. The normal ring eye can straighten out under enough strain.

For the really heavy offshore specialties—marlin, shark, tuna and monster bottom fish—you must use a big-game hook, forged of extra-thick metal as added protection against straightening. These

Sea Demon big-game hook (Mustad 7731)

can be identified at a glance by their flattened appearance, as well as by size. Naturally, the eyes of big game hooks are also of the heavy-duty type—either a needle-eye or else a ring-eye that has been braised in closed position for strength. "Monster hooks" of this sort may also be used inshore, for such specialties as big tarpon with heavy tackle or shark fishing.

Again, there is considerable latitude when it comes to choosing a specific size for certain types of fishing, and much depends on the size of the bait.

WEEDLESS HOOKS

A word must be said about weedless hooks, as these are important to many freshwater fishermen, and are sometimes used in salt water.

The usual weedless hook is nothing more than a familiar style of hook to which has been added an extension of light wire that protects the point, and helps keep it from snagging on weeds or obstructions.

Some artificial lures—usually spoons and spinners, but often flies, jigs and plugs—come equipped with weed guards.

When an angler buys separate weedless hooks, he normally intends to use them for rigging artificial worms and other plastic baits, but they can be handy, as well, for fishing minnows and other live baits. Usually, you should hook a minnow or other baitfish through the lips when using a weedless hook.

Sizes of weedless hooks are denoted by the standard system given earlier.

Another family of weedless hooks is made weedless by design, rather than by adding a wire weed guard. In most of these, the shank is bent near the eye, so that the point is on the same level as the eye. Therefore, the eye and extreme forward portion of the shank serve as a weed guard. Further snag-proofing is provided by the way in which plastic baits are rigged to these hooks—with the point buried in the body of the soft bait. These hooks are commonly referred to as "worm hooks," although plastic worms can be rigged in weedless fashion—that is, with the point buried—to long-shank hooks of standard patterns as well.

Weedless hooks

Swivels and Snapswivels

Swivels perform two major functions for fishermen: They reduce or prevent line twist, and they serve as handy connectors between line and leader.

All swivels are basically the same in that they have two (or more) eyes with shafts that revolve within a central unit. The major divisions within the basic design are the barrel swivel and the ball-bearing swivel. Both types become snapswivels when they are combined with snaps of any sort that open and close to afford a quick connection to leader or rig.

Three-eyed swivels are used in making specialized rigs, some of which are shown in Chapter 6.

No. 4/0   No. 2/0   No.1   No. 3   No. 5   No. 7   No.10   No.12

Barrel swivels

BARREL SWIVELS

Barrel swivels, because they are inexpensive, get the call for most duties. They can be used for any sort of connection where the potential for line twist is minimal or nonexistent.

Many rigs, such as droppers and multiple-hook setups, could be fashioned without swivels, but the incorporation of swivels can make for easier rigging and more effective presentations as well. An example is the Multi-Purpose Stinger Rig shown in Chapter 8.

Two factors should influence your decision as to what size barrel swivel to buy. The first is size, but the choice certainly is not a critical thing, at least not within a span of only a couple or three sizes. You only have to make sure the swivel is strong enough to withstand the drag pressures to which they will be subjected, and large enough to accommodate the diameter of the lines or leaders with which they will be used.

Barrel swivels are sized by exactly the same weird numerical system as are hooks: that is, large numbers mean small swivels. As the numbers get smaller the swivel gets larger—up to a No. 1. At that point, the "o" system kicks in, and the number designations start to rise—the range being from 1/0 to a huge 12/0.

Most casting and light-line applications, whether with spinning or revolving-spool tackle, can be covered with No. 12, 10 or 8 swivels. General angling with light tackle (lines up to 30-pound test) calls for No. 8 up to about No. 1 or 1/0. The heaviest applications, with rods and reels, will require swivels no bigger than 1/0 to 3/0. The really big swivels are designed for use with heavy handlines, outrigger lines and such.

The other choice you have is in color or finish—and that matters but little unless you fish in situations where toothy fish might possibly mistake your bright swivel for the flash of a small baitfish and cut your line. If that's a consideration—and it usually is in salt water—choose swivels with a dull black finish. If black cannot be found, brass is probably less visible to fish than silver, especially after it tarnishes a bit.

Unfortunately, using a dull swivel only reduces the risk of getting your line slashed; it doesn't completely solve the problem. Even black swivels make a tiny wake that can catch the eye of a voracious mackerel or bluefish.

Barrel swivels can reduce line twist to some extent, but their ability to do so vanishes rapidly as load, or pressure, increases. To really attack the problem of line twist when you use lures or rigs that spin a great deal, you have to move up to a higher class of swivel.

Ballbearing swivels

BALLBEARING SWIVELS

These swivels really do have tiny ballbearings in their innards, and you can readily tell it by their performance. However, there is a sharp line of delineation within the ballbearing types.

Typically, imported ballbearing swivels are relatively low in cost. Still, they represent a great improvement over any barrel swivel— so long as the tackle is light and/or the load modest. However, for really demanding work, especially in offshore angling and for the most severe twist challenges, you really should go to an expensive, top-quality, American made ballbearing swivel, such as the Sampo. The price may shock you on first reading but, when absorbed within the overall cost of ocean angling, it's little enough to pay for virtually foolproof reliability.

To mix us up a bit more, ballbearing swivels use a different system of size designation from the barrel-swivel system already discussed. In ballbearing models, a No. 1 is the smallest, and the numbers rise with the size of the swivel. Nos. 1-3 fill the bill for casting and light trolling. Nos. 3-5 are mid-range sizes for general use. Nos. 6-8 are the big-game sizes.

SNAPSWIVELS

Several types of snaps are attached to either barrel or ballbearing swivels to turn them into snapswivels.

Snapswivels serve definite purposes—one of which is NOT to be tied routinely to the end of every fishing line, as beginners often seem to think. Who hasn't spotted a tyro, at one time or another, who has a small hook and bit of shrimp or earthworm dangling from the end of a huge snapswivel?

Casters can make fine use of small snapswivels when they fling twisting lures, such as most spoons and many spinners. Those lures are metallic themselves, so the dab of extra metal that a snapswivel puts at their noses is not likely to detract from their appeal. However, with natural bait rigs that pose a spinning problem, it's best to position a swivel or snapswivel somewhere up the line than to stick a snapswivel to your plain hook.

As mentioned, there are several types of snaps, and not all of them are reliable—least of all the common safety-pin type, which often opens at inopportune moments—meaning when you're fighting a tougher-than-usual fish. A better bet for freshwater anglers would be the lock snap, similar in design to the common safety snap, but with a 90-degree bend that fits in a slot for extra resistance to pulling open. Casters who use either the safety or lock snap with rather heavy lines—15 pounds and up—are advised to mash the snaps closed with pliers as a positive guard against failure.

For demanding work in salt water, several excellent types of snap are available. A choice among them can come down merely to personal, or regional, preferences. Atlantic anglers largely stick to the traditional coastlock or tournament snap. Many Pacific Coasters like the McMahon snap. Scattered users of the corkscrew snap may be found anywhere. Some of these snapswivels offer a choice between single-ring and double-ring makeup. Both are strong enough but the double rings often make for easier and more positive rigging.

Size designations in snapswivels generally run the same as for their non-snap counterparts.

Size 1
10 lb. test

Size 2
25 lb. test

Size 3
60 lb. test

Size 4
100 lb. test

Size 5
165 lb. test

Size 6
200 lb. test

Size 8
300 lb. test

Sampo ballbearing snapswivels with coastlock snap.

69

Chapter 4

Baits Rigs & Tackle

Angling Knots
Knots and Wire Wraps

Rules of Good Knot Tying

Reliable knots are vital to fish-catching success—with all kinds of tackle and all sizes of line, from the heaviest to the lightest. What makes a good knot? Always consider these three factors:

1. Select a suitable knot for the purpose.
2. Fashion the knot properly.
3. Always draw the knot down snugly, and with even pressure.

That last is the one step too often neglected by fishermen. The majority of angling knots (especially if tied with monofilament) are almost certain to slip and fail unless they are drawn tight to begin with.

All the knots to be given here are tried-and-true ties for the fisherman. They are not the only ones in common use, by any means, but they do represent a complete selection that covers any and every need in sportfishing.

Even the simplest knot can't be tied just by glancing at an illustration. The proper way to go about learning new knots is to sit down AT HOME with an assortment of lines and leader material, then study the drawings and follow the printed instruction, step by step. A little additional practice during spare moments will assure you of being able to tie the knot you want when you get to the water. Only after you're able to tie your rigs while fishing, and without pausing to scratch your memory, can you really say you "know" your knots.

Let's go back for a moment to point No. 3, and repeat that all knots should be drawn down snugly. With lighter lines, hand pressure alone can be depended on to tighten the knot sufficiently. When you tie heavy monofilament, however, you often have to grip the hook with pliers to obtain sufficient pressure. And when tying heavy monofilament leader directly to a lighter line, you may have to take a couple of wraps around your hand (use a glove or handkerchief to avoid cuts) before you can draw the knot snug.

Also, with heavy monofilaments, the wraps may not "lay up" close together unless you prod them with a fingernail or blunt instrument as you tighten the knot.

No matter what difficulty you might be having with a particular knot, never try bringing it to final form by jerking sharply. If things aren't going right, start all over. If you jerk while making the knot it will probably break on the spot, and if it doesn't then failure is almost sure to come later at a more unwelcome time.

In addition to the following knots, note that crimped sleeves are sometimes used to secure monofilament leader material—particularly in heavy offshore tests. Crimping procedures are the same as will be described later for wire leaders.

THE VIC DUNAWAY UNI-KNOT SYSTEM

This unique system of knot-tying enables you to learn just one simple knot formation and adapt it to virtually any knotty need— everything from tying a hook to light line, all the way to joining lines that vary by 10 times in test.

Not only is this system the first and only unified approach to knot-tying, but it also provides 100 percent knot strength in most of its applications. The few finished ties which do not test a full 100 percent still test consistently at 90 percent or higher. Moreover, the strength of the Uni-Knot isn't diminished when the line is broken with a jerk, rather than with steady pressure. Some knots which test 100 percent on a steady pull will break at 50 or 60 percent if subjected to severe and sudden jolts—such as might be administered by a big fish striking close to boatside, or by the angler himself, if he gets too muscular in trying to set a hook. The Spider Hitch and Palomar are examples of apparently top-strength knots which break all too easily on a severe shock.

The practiced knot-tying expert will simply add the Uni-Knot system to his personal inventory of ties, using elements of it for particular applications, and other knots, at times, for certain specialties.

But for most fishermen, who are looking for the easiest way to handle their knot needs, the Uni-Knot System is the only thing they really need to learn.

The Uni system works beautifully with braided lines as well as monofilament, and is by far the best way to tie those high-strength/small-diameter braided lines covered in the preceding chapter.

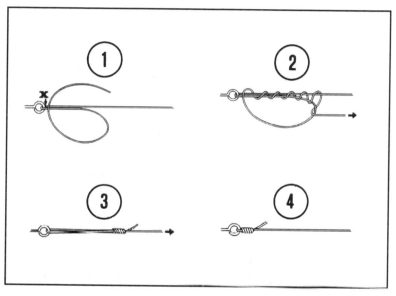

LEARNING THE SYSTEM

The one knot requirement basic to all fishermen is that of tying a line to the eye of a hook or swivel. Familiarize yourself with the simple procedure of using the Uni-Knot for this purpose, and then all other Uni-Knot applications become quite easy.

First, run the line through the eye for several inches. Turn the end back toward the eye to form a circle as shown in picture No. 1. With thumb and finger of the left hand, grasp both strands of line and the crossing strand in a single grip at the point marked just forward of the hook. Now, make six turns with the end around both strands of line and through the circle, as in picture No. 2.

Maintaining the same grip with the left hand, pull on the end of the line in the direction shown by the arrow until all the wraps are snugged tight and close together. Snugging down tightly at this stage is essential to maximum knot strength. If you make six turns and snug the knot very tightly, you'll consistently get 100 percent of line strength.

Finally, slide the finished knot tight against the eye of the hook by dropping the tag end and pulling solely on the standing part of the line as shown by the arrow in picture No. 3. The excess end can be trimmed flush with the knot after final positioning (picture No. 4).

END LOOP

It takes just one slight variation to transform the hook tie into a loop arrangement which provides more freedom of action for artificial lures.

Instead of sliding the finished knot all the way to the eye, just slide it to the size loop desired. Then, gripping the loop just forward of the hook eye, take hold of the tag end with pliers, as shown in picture No. 5, and pull very hard. This locks the Uni-Knot around the standing line (or leader) at that point. If it slides down at all it will only be under heavy pressure when fighting a fish. Meanwhile, the loop position is maintained while casting and retrieving.

LINE TO LINE

Tying line to line is actually done the same way as tying line to hook. Compare picture No. 1 with picture No. 6 and you can see that you handle things the same way, even though the two parallel strands involved are from different pieces of line, rather than from the same piece doubled back.

The procedure is simply to form the Uni-Knot circle with line A around line B, going through six times and pulling down as in picture No. 7. Once the knot is formed and tightened (No. 8), you then have to reverse the lines and tie another Uni-Knot with line B around line A. After the two knots are finished, pull on the two main strands of line, as indicated by arrows in picture No. 9, to slide the two knots together. Trim both excess ends.

This application replaces the Blood Knot, which is one of the most unwieldy of all knots to handle. Breaking strength of this tie is less than 100 percent, but over 90 percent and consistently stronger than the Blood Knot. It can be increased to 100 percent if you double both strands of line before tying the pair of Uni-Knots, but the single tie is strong enough for all practical purposes.

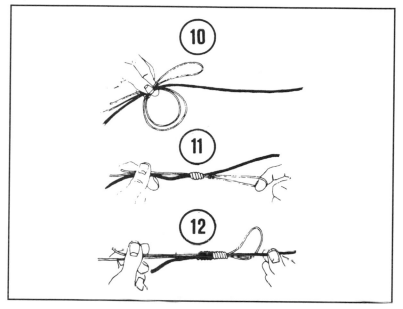

LINE TO LEADER

Tying light line to heavy leader is not much different from the preceding application. It may seem awkward at first because the end of the light line must be doubled to gain maximum strength. But the doubled portion is treated as a single strand and is actually easier to draw down.

Double back several inches of line. Overlap the doubled section with the end of the heavy leader and form the familiar Uni-Knot circle, as in picture No. 10. Go around the strands and through the circle with the doubled end. It is only necessary to go through three times. Now, slip your finger into the loop. Holding all strands on the other side of the knot with the left hand, pull the loop with your finger until the knot is very snug (picture No. 11).

Reverse the lines and tie another Uni-Knot with the end of the heavy leader around both strands of line (there are two strands because the light line is doubled). Again, only three turns are required. Pull the second knot down as snugly as you can manage.

Last, slide the knots together by pulling with opposing pressure on the main strand of leader and both strands of line (picture No. 12). Continue pulling hard until no slippage is felt. For final tightening, you will probably have to grip the line with a full hand grip, instead of using thumb-finger grips.

This tie will consistently provide 100 percent of line strength if the first Uni-Knot is snugged completely tight, and if final tightening is done carefully and with steady hard pressure.

As with all other monofilament knots, improper tying reduces strength.

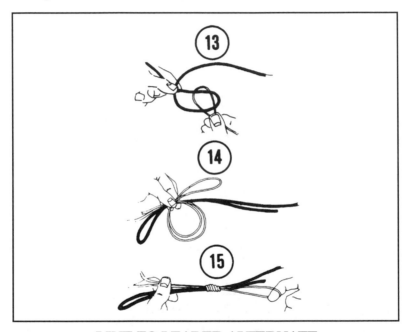

LINE TO LEADER ALTERNATE

This is a different line-to-leader tie that can be used only when diameters of the two monofilaments involved vary by five times or more in test. It makes a much trimmer tie than the previous one if you need to use extremely thick leader. And note that it should be used only with greatly differing diameters, since the bulk of the larger leader is the only thing that can provide a positive hold.

Double both the light line and heavy leader. Insert the doubled line through the leader loop upward, as in picture No. 13. Make the Uni-Knot circle, grip all strands with thumb and finger (No. 14) and then make four turns through the circle. Holding all strands with the left hand, insert finger in loop of light line and draw the Unit-Knot down very tight (No. 15) around both strands of heavy leader.

Last step is to take a firm grip on both strands of light line but only the main strand of leader and pull until the knot slides to the doubled end of the leader. Continue pulling hard until no more slippage is felt, then trim off all excess ends.

Key to successful tying of this one is pulling the knot down completely tight before sliding it to the end. If you feel it's sliding too easily, the knot probably isn't tight enough, and it should be retightened before pulling it to final position.

Done properly, this also is a consistent 100 percent tie, and can be used with seemingly incredible variations in size—for instance, one-pound-test line to 100-pound-test leader.

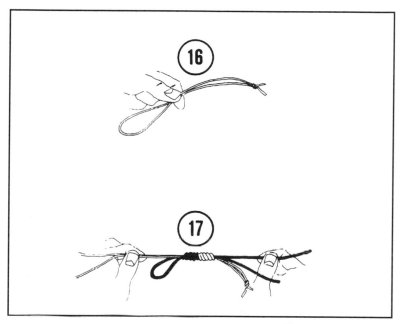

REPLACING THE BIMINI TWIST

To form a maximum strength double-line, you must use a simple but back-door approach. First you cut off enough line to form the desired length of double line, and tie the ends together with an overhand knot as shown in picture No. 16. Then you proceed to tie the double-line back onto your line. The overhand knot is for convenience only and will be trimmed away later.

Double the end of the standing line. The procedure that follows is just the same as the line-to-line tie illustrated with pictures No. 6 through 9. The obvious and only difference is that you're working with two double strands instead of two single strands.

There is one idiosyncrasy, however, that must be catered to in order to get a 100 percent result. After the two knots are pulled together until they just touch, the final tightening must be done by pulling with both strands of double-line, but only the main strand of regular line, as in picture No. 17.

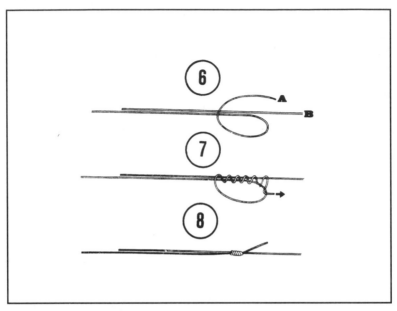

REPLACING THE NAIL KNOT

You can tie a leader to your fly line in seconds with the Uni-Knot, achieving the identical result as with the tedious Nail Knot that requires a tapered nail or tube for tying.

Again, refer to pictures 6 through 8, but assume that line B is your fly line and line A is your leader.

The formation doesn't change at all. However, when you pull the leader knot down around the fly line, you'll have to do it in three or four stages, prodding the wraps together with your thumb in between the stages. This is because the fly line's soft coating does not allow the wraps to be pulled together in a single sweep.

Once you have pulled and prodded the wraps together, getting a result similar to that shown in picture No. 8, grasp the tag end of the leader with pliers. Holding the main strand of leader with your left hand, pull hard with the pliers to make the knot "bite" into the fly line's coating. This is what holds the knot in place. A second Uni-Knot isn't necessary. Trim off the excess ends of leader and fly line as close to the knot as possible, and you have the neatest of all fly leader ties, done in a few seconds.

SNELLING A HOOK

Snelling is a snap with the Uni-Knot. Thread line through the hook eye, pulling through at least six inches. Form the familiar Uni circle and hold it tight against the hook shank with thumb and finger. Make several turns (four or five are enough) around the shank and through the circle. Pull on tag end to draw knot roughly closed. Finish by holding the standing line in one hand, the hook in the other, and pulling in opposite directions.

SPOOLING LINE

To affix line to a revolving spool reel for filling, pass the end of the line around the spool, grasp the tag end and the standing line with thumb and finger of left hand, and tie a Uni-Knot (or you could tie the knot first, leaving a large loop that you simply slip over the spool). Trim the knot close, then pull gently on the standing line to snug the loop tight to the spool.

For a spinning reel spool, simply make a large loop in the end of the line with a Uni-Knot, drop the loop over the spool, and draw it up by pulling on the standing line. In either case, use only two or three wraps to form the Uni.

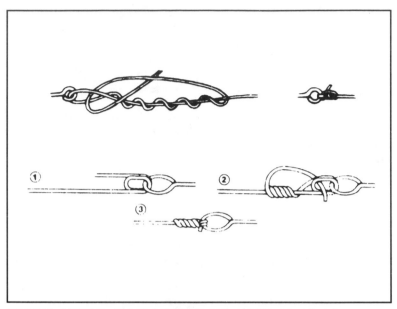

IMPROVED CLINCH, TRILENE KNOTS

The improved clinch long has been the most widely used of all fishing knots, and works well with either monofilament or braided line. Use it for tying line directly to hook, swivel and certain artificial lures, such as jigs, spinners or any lure with a split-ring permanently attached to the lure-eye. Plugs and spoons work best with a loop knot. A lot of fishermen also prefer a loop when using lead-head jigs.

To tie the Improved Clinch, first thread the line through the hook eye, leaving several inches of excess line to work with.

Wrap the end portion around the standing part of the line five times. Fewer wraps weaken the knot; more wraps are unnecessary.

Next, bring the end back toward the hook and insert it through the opening between the hook and the first wrap.

Now turn the end upward again and insert it through the large loop created by the preceding step.

Hold on to the end as you begin to draw the knot tight by pulling on the hook and the line simultaneously. As soon as you're sure the end will not back out of the large loop, you can turn loose and finish the job of drawing tight.

The loose end should be trimmed to about an eighth-inch in length. It should not be trimmed flush with the knot.

The Trilene knot is a simple variation of the Clinch in which the tag end is run through the eye twice (1) and then passed through the resulting double opening just forward of the eye (2). Going through the eye twice, regardless of the knot used, will improve the knot strength of any line.

THE END-LOOP KNOT

This knot can be used for tying a lure to the end of monofilament leader material that is heavier than your line. It is a fast knot to tie, and it affords the necessary freedom of lure action which is so vital to the productivity of many plugs. Do not use this knot for tying a lure directly to light line, because it weakens the line-test too much. Instead, use the TWO-WRAP HANGMAN'S KNOT, which will be described next, or the UNI-KNOT LOOP.

First, and before you put the line through the eye of the lure, tie a simple overhand knot several inches from the end, but do not close the overhand knot at this point.

Second, go through the lure eye, turn, and insert the end of the line through the wide portion of the overhand knot.

The exact size of the final loop is determined at this stage by drawing the overhand knot as close to the lure as you want it.

Finally, make a simple half-hitch with the end of the line around the standing part of the line ABOVE the overhand knot. Pull tight with pressure on the lure and on the line.

Trim, leaving about an eighth-inch end.

PERFECTION LOOP

This knot is used mostly for making loops in the butt end of fly leaders, so that leaders can quickly be changed or replaced. The drawings are in condensed style so that the formations are shown more easily. For convenience, leave yourself a longer length of tag end than shown in the drawings.

A. Form a loop in the end of the mono, making sure it crosses

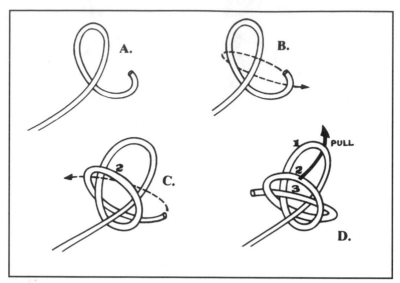

behind the standing portion, as shown. With the thumb and fore-finger of left hand (assuming a right-handed tier) grip the crossing point firmly.

B. Take a turn with the tag end around the front of the loop, creating a second loop, which you incorporate into the same thumb-finger grip.

C. Lay the tag end straight across, between the loops.

D. Holding the whole works in your left hand's thumb-finger grip, take hold of the second loop with fingers of your right hand and slip it through the first loop, as shown by the arrow.

Continuing to pull on this same loop will form and tighten the final knot.

THE TWO-WRAP HANGMAN'S KNOT

This knot is sometimes called the figure eight knot; however, it is different from another and more commonly-used knot which is also called the figure-eight, but which can be used only with certain types of wire. (See chapter on Wire Wraps for that one.)

The Two-Wrap Hangman's Knot results in a slipping loop, which can be tightened at any point to provide the size loop-opening desired. The loop will remain open while casting, but will close tight against the eye when a fish is being fought. After the catch, it can easily be opened again (better retied if the leader has been frayed even slightly).

This knot can be used with either heavy or light monofilament, and is preferable to the End-Loop Knot (described previously) when no heavy leader is being used, because it retains a much higher per-centage of breaking test.

First, thread the line through the eye, allowing yourself several

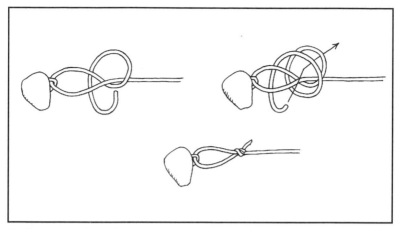

inches to work with.

Now make two wraps back toward the lure-eye (not away from the eye as with the Improved Clinch). Keep these two wraps as loose as possible—holding them open with thumb and finger.

Next, thread the end of the line back through the two wraps, away from the lure-eye and parallel to the standing line.

To tighten this knot it is now necessary to stick the lure into something rigid (such as a boat cleat, tree branch, etc.). After the hook is so fixed, grip the excess end of line with a pair of pliers.

Now pull simultaneously on the line with your hand, and on the excess end with the pliers. You'll note that the knot now slips up and down. Position the loop as you want it, then tighten firmly with extra pressure from the pliers.

Trim, leaving an eighth-inch end.

SURGEON'S KNOT

This is a fast, easy and reliable knot for tying a heavy monofilament leader, or shock line, directly to either monofilament or braided fishing line. It can be used for line and leader of greatly differing diameter, although the practical limit is roughly five times line test—that is, 4-lb. line to 20-lb. leader; 8-lb. to 40-lb.; 10-lb. to 50-lb., etc.

If your diameters differ more than that, it will probably be better to use the Albright Special.

Even though this is one of the easiest of all knots to tie, it is difficult to illustrate plainly. So don't be alarmed. Follow both the illustration and instruction, and you'll be tying it in a few seconds.

First, lay out the leader parallel to the line, letting the end of the line and the end of the leader overlap for six or eight inches.

Now, treating both strands as one, tie a simple overhand knot in the doubled section, making sure that both the short end (line) and long end (leader) are pulled completely through. Do not tighten the knot at this point.

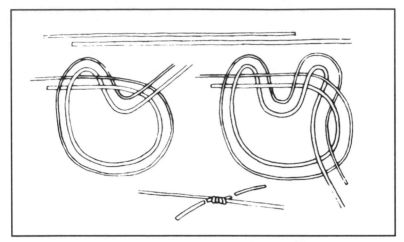

Next, simply go through again with both ends, exactly as before, again making certain both ends are pulled through.

Finally, draw the knot tight by gripping BOTH STRANDS on either side of the knot, and drawing down with steady pressure.

The ends of this knot may be trimmed flush with the wraps.

WORLD'S FAIR KNOT

This easy-to-tie knot tests nearly 100 percent. It got its name from being introduced at the Knoxville World's Fair in 1982 as the winning entry in duPont Stren's "Great Knot Search." To tie, pass the doubled end through the eye (1) and fold it back (2). Next, run the tag end under the doubled strands and over the loop (3). Finally, run the tag end through the loop formed by step 3 (4) and draw tight (5).

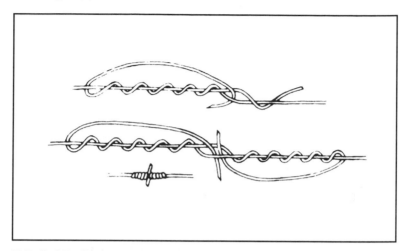

BLOOD KNOT

Best uses for the Blood Knot are to retie a broken spinning line, to add more line to your reel spool, or to join tapered sections of fly fishing leaders. In other words, the Blood Knot is useful mainly for joining together monofilaments of the same, or only slightly differing, diameters.

First, overlap both sections of line, end to end, and then wrap one section around the other five times.

Next, wrap the remaining end around the other section—also five times but in the opposite direction.

Now insert both ends back through the center opening, again in opposite directions.

The knot is pulled tight by drawing on the lines at either side of the knot. Care must be taken at this point to prevent the ends from backing out of the center insert.

Trim, leaving an eighth-inch end.

ALBRIGHT SPECIAL

When you wish to tie a light monofilament line directly to a very heavy monofilament leader (for instance, 10-lb. to 80-lb.) this is the knot to master. It has the added advantage of being a slim and neat tie that will generally slip through the rod guides so you can crank the knot past the rod tip.

The Albright Special also is used for tying light line directly to wire cable, nylon-coated wire or even to single-strand wire leader in the smaller diameters.

This knot is tricky at first, and may take some practice. However, it really isn't very difficult once you get the hang of it.

First, double back a couple inches of the heavy material.

Insert the line through the loop which is thus formed. Pull 10 or 12 inches of line through to give yourself ample line to work with.

Now you must wrap the line back over itself, and over both strands of the doubled leader. While doing this, you are gripping the line and both leader strands together with the thumb and finger of your left hand, and winding with your right. Make 15 turns, then insert the end of the line back through the loop once more at the point of the original entry.

Before turning loose your thumb-and-finger grip, pull gently on the standing part of the line to remove slack; then pull gently on the short end of the leader to close the loop; then pull gently on the short end of the line to remove more slack.

Finally comes the last stage of tightening. Pull the short end of the line as tight as you possibly can. Then pull the standing part of the line tight.

Clip off the excess line, leaving about an eighth-inch end. Clip off the excess from the leader loop, again leaving a very slight protrusion.

SPECIAL NOTE: The Albright Special, in particular, is a knot which must be tied with great care. Practice it thoroughly at home. But, as mentioned before, once you learn it, it seems surprisingly quick and simple.

TUBE OR NAIL KNOT

This one is used to tie a leader butt directly to your fly line. Originally, a nail was used to tie this knot—with the leader being inserted in the small space between nail and line.

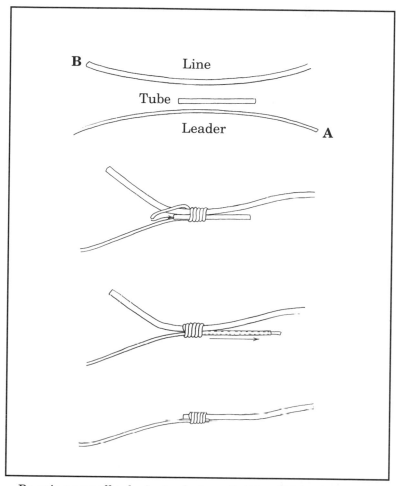

By using a small tube instead of a nail, it is much easier to insert the leader back underneath all the wraps. Any small-diameter tube can be used—a hypodermic needle, the refill barrel of a ballpoint pen (cleaned out, of course), etc.

First, lay out the fly line and leader as in illustration. Grip all three with thumb and finger of left hand.

Take the leader at point A with your right hand, and wrap back toward the end of the fly line (B), making five snug wraps.

Now, run the end of the leader (A again) back through the tube.

Slide the tube out in the direction of the arrow, and tighten the knot by pulling on both ends of the leader. Pull the leader down very tight—using pliers to grip the short end if necessary.

Do not pull on the fly line until after the leader is pulled down so tightly that it bites into the coating of the fly line!

Once the knot is tight, the excess end of the fly line, and of the leader, can be trimmed short.

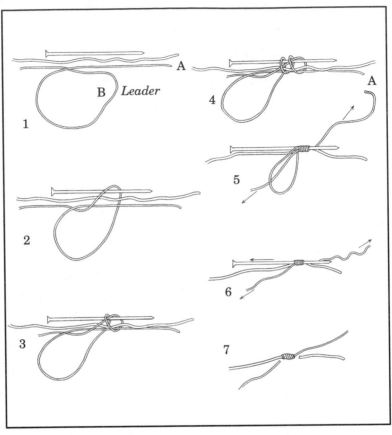

FAST NAIL KNOT

These instructions outline a new and drastically-improved method for tying the Nail Knot. The knot itself is used to tie a permanent leader butt onto the end of a fly line (for instructions on making fly-fishing leaders see Chapter 3).

The preceding method of tying this knot required the use of a specially tapered nail, or a small hollow tube—and the tying consumed several minutes, even if the angler was completely familiar with the procedure.

With this method, you can use any small-diameter object—a nail, needle, or even a match stick or toothpick. It serves only as a "stiffener" to make wrapping easier.

First, make a circle with the leader, as shown in the illustration. Using the thumb and forefinger of your left hand, take all the components in a single grip—nail, fly line, and both overlapping ends of the leader.

Now you do not wrap with any of the ends. You wrap instead with the right-side arc of the leader circle. Grasp this about in the middle (B) with your right hand, and make five snug turns simultaneously around the nail, the fly line and the leader, working back toward your left hand.

When the five turns have been made, let your left thumb-and-finger grip slide over the wraps to hold them tight.

Now use your right hand to grasp the leader end (A) and pull it all the way through until the circle is closed and the knot comes tight.

Remove the nail, and finish tightening the knot by pulling on both ends of the leader. Take care that when you remove the nail, the fly line doesn't slide out of the wraps as well.

As a last step, tighten the knot some more. Use pliers to get a good grip on the short end of the leader. The knot must be pulled tight enough so that it presses firmly into the coating of the fly line.

With clippers, trim the short end of the leader and the short end of the line as close as you can to the knot.

THE "BIMINI TWIST"

The Bimini Twist (also called the Bimini Knot) has long been employed by big-game fishermen to form along double-line in accordance with regulations of the International Game Fish Association.

The value of the double line in big-game fishing is this: When a fish has been brought to boat side, the double line is by then wrapped for a few turns onto the reel. This means that twice the pressure can be applied to keep the fish from bolting, and also that the angler has twice the margin of protection against line breakage at the critical gaffing stage.

In later years, the Bimini Twist was widely adopted by spin, plug and fly fishermen—not to provide a long length of double-line, but to assure maximum possible knot strength. A properly-tied Bimini Twist maintains 100 percent of line strength.

Normally, the light-tackle folks use the Bimini to make no more than two or three feet of double line. This doubled line then is tied directly to the leader (using such knots as the appropriate Uni-Knot ties, the Albright Special or Surgeon's Knot) or else to a swivel (using the Uni-Knot or Improved Clinch Knot).

Any fisherman's knot can be tied with a double line as easily as with a single line.

For most freshwater and inshore fishing, where line-test is reasonably well matched to the fish generally encountered, it is not necessary to rig with the double line. All the Uni-Knot ties afford nearly 100 percent strength, while knots such as the Surgeon's and Improved Clinch afford 85 or 90 percent.

On the other hand, a Bimini Twist double-line should always be used with any kind of tackle and in any kind of fishing where your line is likely to be put to the full test of its strength. Following are a few examples: all offshore fishing; tarpon fishing with fly, plug or spin tackle, or with light general tackle; snook fishing in tight quarters, such as mangrove creeks or around pilings; all kinds of saltwater fly casting where a heavy tippet is employed; deep jigging and other deep-sea, light-tackle specialties.

TYING THE BIMINI TWIST

This is one knot which really is difficult for the fellow who hasn't tied it before. But, once learned, it can be tied in less than a minute—and take heart at the knowledge that hundreds of fishermen now tie it routinely and quickly, even in a rocking boat. You can too, if you practice and master it at home.

The one most important thing to remember when tying the Bimini is to keep pressure at all times on all three points—1. The standing line above the knot. 2. The end of line which you're working with. 3. The terminal end of the loop.

Photo No. 1—Double the end of your line, making the doubled portion about three feet long. Insert your hand in the loop and make 20 complete revolutions with your hand to form the 20 wraps. Note that at this stage, the wraps are spread over a considerable portion of the line.

Photo No. 2—Sitting erect, hold your knees tightly together and place the loop over them. Maintain pressure, as shown, with your hands on both the standing line and the short end.

Photo No. 3—Spread your knees slowly, maintaining very tight hand pressure in opposing directions, as before. This will draw the wraps tightly together.

Photo No. 4—Once the wraps are very snug, pull slightly downward with the short end while relaxing tension slightly at the same time. Be sure to keep up the tension, however, with the left hand and with the knees. The line should then roll easily over the wraps, all the way down to the end.

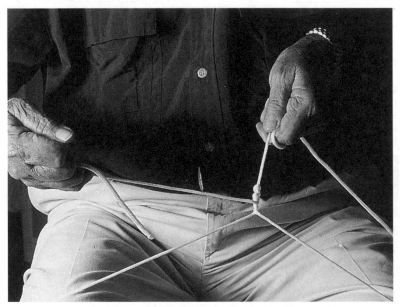

Photo No. 5—This shows the completed rollover before it is anchored with a half-hitch around one strand, and several half hitches around both strands. IMPORTANT NOTE: This photo is somewhat deceiving, in that it shows the rollover wraps lying perfectly parallel and snug against each other. Your finished wrap may show a considerably more spiraled look. This is perfectly O.K., so long as all wraps are tight.

Step No. 6 (Drawing)—This shows detail of finishing half hitches: the first around a single strand, and three others around both strands. Instead of making three separate finishing hitches, you can make just one—and go through it three times with the tag end instead of only once. Trim, leaving about an eighth-inch end.

ADDITIONAL NOTES ON THE ROLLOVER—Obviously, the steps illustrated here are for making a short double line for use with casting tackle. To make 15 or 30 feet of double line for big-game fishing, two people should be involved. One man handles the mechanics of forming the knot, while the other spreads the two strands of double line and maintains tension on them. In short, the second man (with his hands) performs the same function that your knees did while making the short double line.

94

Chapter 5

Baits Rigs & Tackle

Wire Wraps

How to Wrap Fishing Wire

There are several types of fishing wire, and the purpose of this section is merely to give instruction as to how each type should be wrapped onto a hook, lure or swivel.

Instructions on how to choose among the various types and sizes of wire, and their uses as fishing leaders, are covered in Chapter 3.

These are the types of wire in regular use:

1. Stainless steel single-strand leader wire.
2. Monel single-strand trolling wire (wire line).
3. Wire cable, formed of twisted wire filaments, for leaders.

4. Wire cable, coated with plastic, for leaders.

Every type comes in a great range of diameters. When working with single-strand wire, all diameters are wrapped in exactly the same way; however, the larger the wire, the more difficult it will be to wrap. When working with the larger sizes, it will be necessary to grip your loops of wire with pliers as you make the wrap.

Cutting pliers, obviously, are a necessity when working with wire. They will be needed to cut the desired length of wire from your coil or spool. In some cases (mostly with cable) cutters are used to trim the end after the wrap. But single-strand wire should be BROKEN, not cut, or a tiny sharp end will be left, which can rip a careless hand.

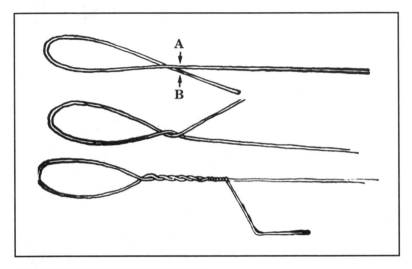

THE HAYWIRE TWIST

For top strength and reliability, the Haywire Twist should be the standard wrap with single-strand leader wire or Monel wire line in virtually all types of saltwater fishing. Experience has DEFINITE-LY PROVED that simple overhand wire wraps will invariably pull out under heavy pressure. For light inshore fishing with spinning tackle, the overhand wrap will usually hold up—but even there you run the risk of losing an exceptional fish due to prolonged strain.

Though instructions are given for the overhand wrap, it is strongly recommended that everyone learn the Haywire Twist and use it as common practice for any kind of wire-leader fishing.

Here's how it's done:

Start by forming the desired size loop. You may simply make a loop for later attachment to a snap, or you may run the wire through the eye of hook or swivel. In either case, the procedure is the same.

Cross the strands as shown. Hold loop tightly with fingers of left hand, or with pliers. Using right hand, press DOWN at point A with forefinger, and at the same time press UP at point B with thumb.

The second illustration shows how the wire should look after the first twist. Using exactly the same procedure, repeat three or four times if making a wire leader, or 10 to 12 times if wrapping Monel trolling wire.

After making the series of Haywire Twists, finish off by wrapping the short end around the standing wire as snugly as possible several times. This finishing wrap does not add strength, but is necessary to keep the Haywire from unwrapping. Unless the wraps (called barrels) are snugged tightly against each other, you will have trouble breaking the wire, as described next.

BREAK THE WIRE by bending a "crank handle" in the surplus end, as shown. Then, while holding the loop tightly in the left hand, crank this handle in a full circular motion. The surplus will snap off neatly at the last wrap.

If you have difficulty breaking the wire in this manner it is probably because you are making the circular motion in the same direction as you made the wrap. You must let your circular sweep run PARALLEL to the standing part of the wire—not AROUND the standing wire. One way to make sure you are cranking in the right direction is to make your circle in such a way as to let the "elbow" of your little handle brush the standing part of the wire as it goes by.

OVERHAND WIRE WRAP

The Overhand Wrap is nothing more than the final stage of the Haywire Twist. You merely run the end of the wire through the hook eye, then bend it back and wrap the short end around the long end several times.

Finish off by breaking the wire as directed previously.

THE GREENE TWIST

This wire twist, amazing as it seems, gives an extra measure of breaking safety over the traditional Haywire Twist. This extra margin means little in routine angling, especially with light and medium tackle, and when fish are netted or gaffed. However, in big-game fishing, when the leader must be handled by a mate to bring

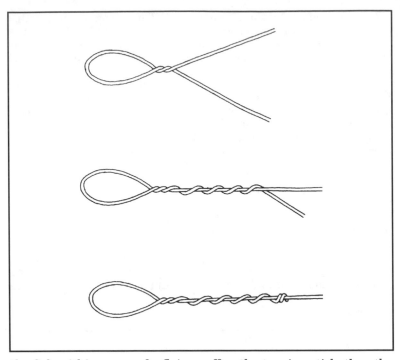

the fish within range of a flying gaff or the tagging stick, then the Greene Twist is a surer bet to withstand the extra pressure.

First form the loop or run the wire through the hook eye, as the case may be, and then begin the wrap exactly the same as for the Haywire; however, you make only two Haywire wraps. Next, wrap the tag end around the standing wire five or six times very loosely —so loosely that it would unwind if you let it go. Last, complete with two—and two only—overhand wraps as with the Haywire, and break off the tag end.

THE QUICK-CHANGE WIRE WRAP

Here is a useful wrap for the fellow who casts with light spinning or baitcasting tackle and likes the convenience of fast lure change.

You start out as if making the regular overhand wrap, but you spiral the wraps widely four or five times instead of making tight barrels.

You won't be able to break off the surplus but must cut it off with pliers: however, if you're careful to cut right on the last bend, the danger of being stuck by the sharp end is lessened. Even so, keep your hands away from the wraps, except when changing lures.

To change lures, unwrap the wide spirals, put on the new lure, and wrap the whole thing closed again. It takes but a few seconds.

Though not as reliable as a Haywire, the wide spiral twist is surprisingly strong—much stronger than the tight overhand.

SPECIAL SPOON WRAP

Here's a nifty system for attaching a trolling spoon to your wire leader. It gives the spoon much more action in the water, and is widely used by commercial kingfishermen and by guides.

Run your leader wire through the eye of the spoon, pulling several inches of wire through. Turn the end of the wire and go through the eye again, same way as before.

Now you see that a circle of wire has been formed. Run the end of your wire in and out through this circle several times, until you go completely around the circle and get back to the standing part of the leader wire. Now make your Haywire Twist, finish with the barrel regular wrap and break off the surplus wire as usual.

NOTE: Immediately after forming the circle, adjust the size of the circle to desired diameter by pulling on the loose end of wire. The diameter usually is about a half-inch.

Rigging Multi-Strand Wire (Cable)

Multi-strand twisted wire is commonly used for leader material in both light tests for inshore fishing, and heavy tests for big-game application. Some braided wire has a nylon coating.

There are no strict rules to follow in choosing between multi-strand and single-strand wire for your metallic leaders, although general guidelines are offered at the beginning of the chapter on "Leaders."

All but one of the connections to be described here may be used with either plain or nylon-coated cable. The one exception is the match method, usable only with nylon coating.

SLEEVE AND CRIMPER

This is probably the most widely used method of attaching cable leaders—light or heavy—to a hook, trolling lure or swivel. Sleeves can also be used to make monofilament leaders, but they seldom are—except in heavy tests for offshore trolling. Sizes of both the sleeves and crimping tools (crimping pliers) vary widely and are sold at many tackle shops specializing in saltwater gear. Sleeves must be chosen to match the diameter of the wire or monofilament you plan to use. Any dealer who sells sleeves should have a chart detailing appropriate sizes for the brands and tests he stocks.

When using large sleeves on heavy monofilament leaders, special (and expensive) crimping devices are available that provide a positive crimp, yet do not bruise and weaken the leader material.

SINGLE SLEEVE RIG—One sleeve may be used with light cable wire for light-duty fishing. To rig, simply thread the sleeve onto the wire, then run the end of the wire through the eye of your hook, and then back through the sleeve. Adjust to the desired size loop, crimp the sleeve, and trim off excess wire.

DOUBLE SLEEVE RIG—For added protection against failure (and especially with larger sizes of cable), use two sleeves. Start by crimping on the first sleeve as described in the preceding paragraph. Then wrap the excess end once or twice around the standing part of the leader and thread it through a second sleeve. Last, crimp the second sleeve and trim off excess wire.

CIRCLE WRAP WITH DOUBLE SLEEVE FOR HEAVY BIG GAME FISHING—This type of connection is the choice of many big-game fishermen who seek the largest marlin with 80- or 130-pound-test line and either wire cable leader or monofilament testing 200 pounds or more. It provides maximum protection against weakening and breaking during a high-pressure fight that could easily last several hours. Anglers who like wire for this application choose heavy cable over heavy single strand-wire because it is not apt to kink and snap. The connection is made by running the leader TWICE through the eye of hook or swivel. This forms a circle of wire. Run the end of the wire through the circle (the circle should be small—1/2-inch or less in diameter) three or four times, or until the end of the wire gets back to the standing part. Now wrap the end once around the leader, slip the first sleeve over this wrap, and crimp it. Last, wrap the end three or four times around the leader and crimp on the second sleeve. (NOTE: For detail drawing on how to form the wire circle, see the illustration entitled SPOON WRAP in the section on rigging single-strand wire.)

FIGURE-EIGHT KNOT

Light cable or nylon-covered cable may be tied directly to lure hook or swivel by using this simple yet strong knot. You merely wrap the end once around the leader, then thread it back through the first opening—as shown in the illustration. Use pliers to hold the end as you pull the knot tight.

101

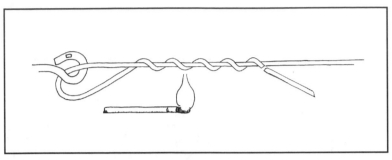

THE MATCH METHOD

A simple system for securing nylon-coated cable to a hook or swivel is shown in the illustration. Run the end through the eye, then wrap it three or four times around the leader. Leave a couple of inches excess so you can hold the wraps in place without getting your fingers close to the fire. Now strike a match and pass the flame quickly back and forth along the wraps until the nylon melts and fuses. Do not hold the flame against the wraps too long or the nylon will melt away completely! After fusion is complete, trim off the excess end of wire.

TYING CABLE TO MONOFILAMENT

Cable or nylon-coated cable in the smaller diameters can be tied directly to monofilament line or leader by using the Albright Special Knot. Simply double the wire end about one inch, then tie the Albright as described in an earlier section.

WIRE LEADER SIZES (CABLE)

Table is for Sevenstrand

Size (pound test)	Diameter
18	.011
27	.012

40	.015
60	.018
90	.024
135	.029
170	.033
250	.039

WIRE LEADER SIZES
(NYLON-COATED CABLE)
Table is for Sevalon

Size (pound test)	Diameter
18	.018
27	.020
40	.024
60	.034
90	.048
135	.058
170	.065
250	.075

WIRE LEADER SIZES
(SINGLE-STRAND)

No.	Diameter	Lb. Test
2	.011	28
3	.012	32
4	.013	39
5	.014	54
6	.016	61
7	.018	72
8	.020	88
9	.022	108
10	.024	127
12	.029	184
15	.035	258
19	.043	352

WIRE LEADER SIZES
(AIRCRAFT CABLE)
Table is for Duratest

Size (pound test)	Diameter
175	.036
275	.042
400	.053
600	.067
800	.092

104

Chapter 6

Baits Rigs & Tackle

Leaders and Rigs

Tips on Leader Selection

Fishing leaders can be divided into two broad classes:

1. Leaders designed for lowest possible visibility, so that the lure or bait looks, to the fish, as if it isn't connected to anything.

2. Leaders designed to protect the line from shock, abrasion, sharp teeth, or from being cut by the fins or tail of exceptionally large fish.

The perfect leader would be one which is virtually invisible, yet strong enough to resist even the jaws of a bluefish or barracuda. Unfortunately, there is no kind of leader material which comes close to providing the advantages of both extremes; therefore, any leader you make up, for any kind of fishing, is necessarily compromised to some extent.

Low-visibility leaders are generally used in freshwater fishing, and in a few saltwater situations where the water is clear and the prey spooky. In fact, for the great majority of freshwater fishing the angler needs no leader at all, IF he is using monofilament line. The line serves as its own low-visibility leader, and nothing heavier is usually needed. However, the angler who uses braided line is advised to use a simple monofilament leader for reduced visibility, even if the breaking test is the same as that of his line. He can, of course, use either lighter or heavier mono as conditions dictate.

But there are many freshwater occasions when a monofilament leader heavier than the line is called for. Even the small teeth of a bass might wear through extremely light line (say 6-pound-test and under), and so the ultra-light angler may find it advisable to tie on a mono leader of around 12- or 15-pound-test in some instances. With lines of 8- to 15-pound-test (the usual size range for most freshwater fishing) it pays to employ a 20- or 30-pound-test monofilament leader when fishing in or near thick weeds. It's also a good idea to use the heavy leader when live-baiting for bass, unless your line tests 20 pounds or more. Bass often swallow a bait deep, and if you hook the big one you're always hoping for, he just might manage to fray your 10- or 12-pound line before you can get him to the net.

All fly-fishing leaders, of course, fall into the low-visibility classification. A fly line is very thick, and so a monofilament leader must be used to form a less visible connection to the fly. Sometimes (mainly in salt water) additional protection is also needed at the fly, and this is accomplished through a heavy tippet, attached to the regular thin fly leader.

Except when fishing for gar and larger members of the pike- pickerel clan, the freshwater angler is not apt to need a mono leader heavier than 30 pounds, or a wire leader. But leaders designed for protection, rather than low visibility, are necessary in just about every area of saltwater fishing.

MONOFILAMENT OR WIRE?

Monofilament leaders should get first call over wire in the great majority of applications. Use wire only in cases where monofilament can easily be cut, such as by the teeth of bluefish, mackerel or barracuda. Even then, monofilament will usually result in more strikes, and so you will have to judge for yourself whether the switch to wire is likely to produce enough additional catches to justify it. In a "hot bite," wire probably will not be a disadvantage.

Snapper, grouper and sea trout (weakfish) are a few examples of fish which possess formidable-looking teeth, yet they do not seriously threaten monofilament leaders because their teeth are not designed for shearing or clipping. Monofilament is a better choice than wire for any of those species.

A few species, though possessing no visible teeth, own exceptionally raspy or bony jaws. This group includes the tarpon and snook. Monofilament leaders can and should be used for both species (when casting, anyway), but it must be heavy enough to withstand the raspy jaws over a considerable length of time. Mono as heavy as 100-pound-test is needed when seeking large tarpon—say 75 pounds and heavier. For smaller tarpon, and for snook, 40- to 60-pound leaders are about right, while 30-pound-test is the minimum practical size, even for snook that average less than 10 pounds.

Why not use thinner wire, rather than thicker monofilament, for such fish as snapper, grouper, tarpon or snook? Because it seems obvious from the cumulative experience of many anglers that even the thinnest wire is more likely to spook a fish than is monofilament of considerably greater diameter. Also, the supple monofilament is not subject to some of the pitfalls that accompany the use of wire—kinking, spiraling, etc. And an important benefit for the caster is the fact that the soft mono allows much better action with almost every sort of artificial lure.

Wire is less objectionable when trolling than when casting—possibly because most fish approach a trolled bait from the rear, or possibly because the wake of the boat helps camouflage the leader.

CHOOSING WIRE MATERIAL

In those instances where wire leader is a necessity, the angler still must select between single-strand wire and cable or twisted wire. Another option is cable which has been coated with nylon.

Though single-strand wire is the most popular, there are no ready rules to help you in making your own selection. The only thing that can be done here is to discuss the merits and demerits of each, and mention a few popular applications.

Single-strand stainless leader wire is less expensive than cable. It also is faster and easier to secure, and is more readily adaptable to rigging a variety of baits. Thus, single-strand is the overwhelming choice of both charter boatmen and private anglers who do a lot of offshore fishing. It also is widely used (in smaller diameters) for inshore trolling.

The main disadvantage of single-strand wire is that it can kink and seriously weaken the leader. You must inspect it frequently for such kinks, and if any are observed, the kink must be cut out and the leader rewrapped or replaced. Do not attempt to "unkink" the leader by bending it in the opposite direction, as this will weaken it even more. However, minor offset bends which develop in single-strand wire can safely be straightened without appreciable loss of strength.

Cable wire is more supple than single-strand, and so is a logical choice for casters who require a short wire leader. Nylon-covered cable is more supple yet, and you might prefer to use it instead of plain cable—however, sharp-toothed fish can quickly shred the soft coating, and so you may have to change leaders more often.

Heavy cable leaders are still used in some big-game fishing, particularly for sharks. However, heavy monofilament (200-300-pound-test) has largely replaced cable for marlin fishing. At any rate, cable is resistant to kink-breakage, which single-strand wire is not.

LEADER LENGTH AND CONNECTION

For all kinds of casting, the monofilament leader should be tied directly to your line, using the appropriate Uni-Knot, the Surgeon's Knot or the Albright Special. If the line is doubled first with the Bimini Twist, the connection of double-line to leader should prove of 100 percent strength, despite the knot chosen. With single line, the Surgeon's Knot will reduce strength by 15-20 percent, but both the Uni and Albright will hold at 90 percent or better.

Even for the lightest fishing, the mono leader should be at least two feet long. This allows a few inches of leader to be cranked inside the tip guide when you cast, and means that the leader—not the light line—will be absorbing the strain and chafe of the tip during the cast.

Much longer mono leaders are required for certain heavy-duty types of casting, such as surf-fishing and ocean-casting with lures weighing two ounces and up. Your mono must be long enough so that it will go through all the guides and wrap a couple of times around the reel—and still leave the necessary casting length outside the tip guide. This arrangement is sometimes referred to as a "shock line" or "shock leader."

As a matter of fact, this shock-leader arrangement is a good one to use as your basic leader rig for just about every kind of saltwater fishing with spinning tackle or light-line classes (under 30-pound) of general tackle. Here's how it works: Tie several feet of 30- or 40-pound-test monofilament directly to your line. Most of the time this will be all the leader necessary, and because you have a goodly length of it, you can change lures frequently, cutting the leader back a number of times before it gets so short you have to change it.

Now, if you get into toothy fish such as blues, you simply add a short length of wire, 12-18 inches, to the end of your shock leader, using a small black swivel as a connector. If you want to go after big tarpon, tie 12 inches of 80- or 100-pound mono to your shock leader, using the Uni-Knot or Albright Special. Or, when you take a yen for bottom-fishing, slip your sinker onto the shock leader, then tie on a swivel and add the desired length and size of additional leader.

The long shock leader has numerous advantages, of which shock absorption is only one. It acts as a safeguard against a large fish wrapping up in the leader and breaking the line; it guards against a big fish reaching past a short leader and breaking or cutting the line with sweeps of its tail; it better takes the abrasive punishment of underwater obstacles, such as coral or oysters.

MONO LEADER SUGGESTIONS
(For lines of 20-pound-test and under)

Type of Fishing	Leader Length	Leader Test (Pounds)
Most freshwater	2-3'	none to 20
All-around inshore	2' to rod length	20-40
Snook, tarpon	rod length	30-50
Deep jigging, reef or bottom fishing	rod length	50-60
Ocean casting (surface and mid-depth)	rod length	30-60
Ocean trolling (sails, dolphin, etc.)	6-12'	40-80
Ocean Trolling (Marlin)	12-15'	80-300

NOTE: Add a short tippet of 80 or 100-pound mono to your basic leader when fishing for big tarpon. Add a short tippet of wire if likely to be getting strikes from bluefish, mackerel, barracuda, shark. In either case, the tippet should be about 12 inches long.

WIRE LEADER SUGGESTIONS

Type of Fishing Wire	Length	Wire Size
Inshore casting, trolling, light bottom fishing	6" to 3'	2-5
Offshore trolling, drifting (sails, dolphin, etc.)	6-8'	3-7
Offshore trolling (billfish, big tuna)	12-15'	9-12
Bottom fishing, deep trolling	3-9'	7-9
Shark fishing (large shark)	12' to 15'	9 and up

Leaders for Heavy Tackle

STANDARD OFFSHORE LEADER—WIRE

To make line ready for instant attachment or change of leaders first form the desired length of double line, then tie to the end of the double line a heavy-duty snapswivel, preferably ballbearing.

The basic Uni Knot or Improved Clinch Knot may be used to tie the swivel.

Prepare the wire leader by forming a small loop on one end, using the Haywire Twist, and attaching your hook or rigged bait to the other end, also with the Haywire Twist. Refer to the table of Wire Leader Suggestions for size and length of wire.

Several of these leaders can be made up in advance, coiled neatly, and kept ready for quick change simply by unsnapping and re-snapping the snapswivel.

You can either rig your baits to the leaders as needed, or you can rig several baits in advance (leaders and all) and keep them coiled and ready in an ice chest.

You may, of course, use an ordinary swivel instead of a snap swivel. In this case, you would not make the wire loop, but merely leave the end of the leader as is, so it can be wrapped to the swivel.

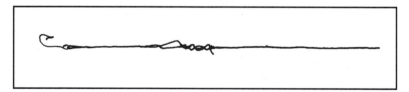

OFFSHORE LEADER— WIRE AND MONOFILAMENT

Quite a few charter boatmen are now using heavy monofilament leaders for offshore trolling—with only 18-24 inches of wire at the end. The short length of wire is ample to guard against cutting by bills or teeth, and it also makes bait-rigging easier. Ballyhoo and some other trolling baits are more difficult or time-consuming to rig with monofilament.

This leader arrangement is especially helpful to anyone who fishes offshore in a small boat, or even a large boat with a cramped cockpit. The monofilament is much easier to control in tight quarters than is a long length of wire, and offers other advantages as well.

Again, start with a snapswivel tied to your double line.

Prepare the monofilament leaders in advance. The monofilament will form all but a couple of feet of your overall leader and can test as little as 40-pounds when you use light lines (20-pound or less)for dolphin, small tuna and sailfish; or anywhere from 100 to 300 pounds when using heavy tackle for marlin.

Using the Improved Clinch Knot or the Two-Wrap Hangman's Knot, tie a stout swivel to one end of the leader; a ballbearing snapswivel to the other.

The short wire tippets can also be prepared in advance, with or without baits. You rig the bait as usual and form a haywire loop in the other end of the short wire, as usual.

Snap the monofilament leader to your line by attaching the plain swivel of the leader to the snapswivel on your line. The wire is then attached to the snapswivel at the other end of the monofilament leader.

Change baits simply by snapping the short wires on and off the monofilament. The heavy mono section of leader seldom needs changing.

OFFSHORE LEADER— HEAVY MONO OR WIRE CABLE

This leader is not illustrated because it consists simply of a single length of heavy monofilament or cable, usually 15 to 30 feet, with a hook rigged to one end and a large swivel to the other. The sleeve-and-crimp method of attaching the hardware is explained in the section on Wire Wraps. Refer to the general discussion on leaders at the beginning of this chapter, for more information on the cable leader. Refer also to the instructions for rigging big-game trolling lures in a later section.

Heavy cable is preferable to single-strand wire leaders for the following fishing specialties: giant marlin, giant swordfish, big sharks, big bottom fish at extreme depth (for instance, Warsaw grouper).

Present-day big-game anglers exhibit a wide preference for heavy monofilament over cable when seeking swordfish, marlin and big tuna, but the option to use cable remains.

Leaders for Light Tackle

(Spin, Baitcasting, Surfcasting, Service Tackle)

ALL-PURPOSE STRAIGHT MONOFILAMENT

This is the simplest of leaders and the most widely useful, con-

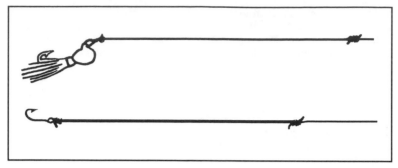

sisting of nothing more than a length of heavy monofilament tied directly to your line.

For freshwater and light saltwater fishing, make the tie with the Uni-Knot.

For any kind of saltwater fishing where your line is apt to be put to the full test of its strength, make a double line first, then tie your leader to the double line, using the Uni-Knot or Albright Special Knot. Only with a double line can you be sure of getting 100 per - cent knot strength.

As indicated by the two illustrations, most lures should be tied to the heavy mono with a Uni-Loop or End Loop Knot. Hooks for fishing with bait should be tied with the standard Unit or Improved Clinch Knot.

Recommended lengths of mono leaders are discussed at the beginning of this chapter. Recommended strengths are shown in a separate table.

MONO LEADER WITH
HEAVY OR WIRE TIPPET

In some cases (as has already been discussed) it is desirable to add an additional short leader of stronger material (called a tippet) to your basic leader.

You can add heavier mono by tying it on with the Uni-Knot or Albright Special Knot.

You can add light cable or nylon-coated cable, by tying it on with the Albright Special OR by using a swivel as a connector. The swivel should be tied to the leader with the Uni or Improved Clinch. The wire tippet must be attached to the swivel by means of the Figure-

Eight Knot or a crimped sleeve.

If you wish to add single-strand wire, a swivel is the best way. Be sure to use the Haywire Twist in wrapping your wire to the swivel.

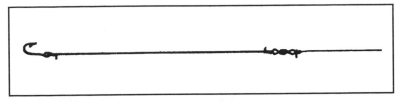

STRAIGHT WIRE LEADERS

With lines under 20-pound-test, it is seldom advisable to use a straight wire leader without a shock leader of monofilament. Though you can often get by without it, the added strength of the shock leader is highly desirable.

However, if you wish to use a wire leader up to three or four feet long, without the shock leader, rig it as follows:

Wrap your wire to a swivel, using the Haywire Twist. Wrap the other end of the wire to your hook or lure, also by means of the Haywire.

If you desire fast lure or bait change, you can use the Quick Change Wrap, which is quite dependable though not quite as strong as the Haywire.

Tie the swivel to your line with the Uni or Improved Clinch Knot.

Sinker Rigs

THE SPLITSHOT

Split-shot sinkers are the smallest type available—and by far the handiest to use. Split-shot require no special leader or rigging but are merely pressed onto whatever rig you're using, if and when a small amount of weight is needed to improve casting ease, or to sink your bait a bit faster.

The splitshot has long been standard in freshwater fishing, but is largely overlooked by saltwater anglers. Yet it can be just as helpful to folks who fish the coast. The saltwater fisherman who keeps splitshot handy will find many instances when he is able to add just the right amount of added weight without having to re-rig with a different type of sinker—which likely as not is bigger than he really needs.

Press the splitshot to your leader, using pliers. The shot is best positioned about six inches from the hook.

If more than one shot is used, do not place them close together but keep them about an inch apart.

CAUTION: Crimping a splitshot directly to light line may severely weaken it at that point. Best use of shot on leaders only.

CLINCH OR RUBBERCOR SINKER

The clinch is a tapered sinker, with a full-length groove and soft "ears" at either end. You attach the clinch simply by laying your leader in the groove of the sinker, folding the "ears" over the line, then pressing the groove closed with pliers.

The Rubbercor is a patented sinker, which works in much the same way as the clinch. But it is a much-improved design and considerably easier to use, because it can be taken off and put on at will—with no pliers and without bruising the line or leader.

Instead of the lead ears, the Rubbercor has a center insert of rubber, which protrudes at both ends of the sinker. You lay your line in the groove, twist the rubber ends and your line is secured. To remove, twist the rubber ends in the opposite direction.

Clinch and Rubbercor sinkers come in various weights, and are especially useful in weights of one-quarter ounce and heavier, where they replace several splitshot.

SLIDING OR EGG SINKER RIG

This is pretty much the standard sinker used for saltwater fishing. Egg sinkers range in size from one-quarter ounce to several ounces, but the basic rig shown here is widely used with all of them —whether you're using a half-ounce sinker on a spinning rod for inshore channel fishing, or a two-ounce sinker on a boat rod for reef bottom fishing.

First you slide the sinker onto your line (or, preferably, your shock leader), then tie on a swivel, using the Uni or Improved Clinch

Knot; then add your leader and hook.

As you can see, the egg sinker is free to travel along your line but is stopped well above your hook by the swivel. When a fish bites, he can take out line without feeling the weight of the sinker.

It is advisable to use a shock leader, or double line, above the swivel, because the free-running sinker often bangs hard against the swivel while you're fishing. If your light line is tied straight to the swivel, your knot might be quickly weakened and a breakoff can occur.

Split shot

EGG SINKER RIG WITH SPLITSHOT STOPPER

The egg sinker can be used without a swivel if you prefer.

If you're using a shock leader tied directly to a heavy tippet simply slide the sinker onto your shock leader before you tie the tippet. The knot will be plenty large enough to assure that the sinker won't slide over it to your hook.

If you wish to use a shock leader without a heavy tippet, slide the egg sinker onto the leader before tying on your hook. Now, if you want to keep the sinker away from your hook, just press a tiny splitshot to your leader at the desired point a foot or so away from the hook to keep the sinker from sliding farther.

VARIATION: Although tradition calls for using a swivel or a splitshot as a "stopper" to keep the sliding sinker separated from the hook, many bottom fishermen now eliminate the stopping device altogether and allow the sinker to slide all the way down to the hook. This arrangement, sometimes called a "Knocker rig," makes for easier casting and, when it's resting on bottom, the closeness of the sinker seldom, if ever, seems to keep fish from biting.

PYRAMID SINKER RIG

The egg sinker just doesn't hold position on smooth bottom, if there is any current or wave action. That's why pyramid sinkers are the standard weights for surf and ocean-pier anglers, who fish mostly over sand.

The rig shown here is built around a three-way swivel: that is, a swivel with three eyes instead of the standard two. Tie your line or shock leader to one eye, using the Uni or Improved Clinch Knot. To the second eye, tie a short piece of heavy monofilament, and to the other end of the monofilament, tie your pyramid sinker. The same knots serve for all those ties.

The third eye, of course, is where you attach your leader, hook and bait. Monofilament generally is the leader choice, but you might wish to use wire if expecting bluefish, shark, etc.

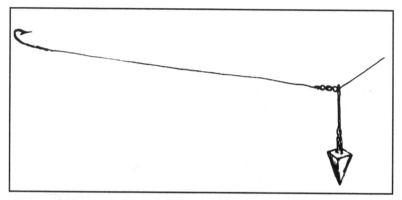

PYRAMID FISH FINDER RIG

The other basic rig for the pyramid sinker is the fish-finder or sliding-sinker arrangement. It works much like the egg sinker rig, in that the pyramid sinker is allowed to slide freely up and down the line or shock leader above your swivel.

This could be accomplished simply by threading your line through the eye of the pyramid sinker, but such an arrangement really isn't satisfactory. You should use a SINKER SLIDE, which can be purchased at most tackle stores in beach country.

The sinker slide is simply a small accessory which has an eye on one end (for your line to run through), and a snap on the other, to which your sinker is attached.

THE TROLLING SINKER

Trolling sinkers generally weigh several ounces and are used mostly with medium or heavy tackle, including wire line outfits, for deep-reef and ocean trolling.

Some trolling sinkers are torpedo-shaped, while others are kidney or keel-shaped to reduce line twist. Some have a planing head which helps attain a greater depth. All have an eye (or bead chain) at either end for ease of rigging.

Regardless of shape, they are all rigged as follows:

1. Tie a heavy-duty swivel to your line or double line.

2. Wrap about three feet of leader wire to the swivel and wrap the other end of the wire to the forward eye of the trolling sinker.

3. Take a second length of leader wire, 3 to 6 feet long as desired. Wrap one end to the rear eye of the trolling sinker, and the other end to your hook or lure.

VARIATION FOR WIRE LINE: If using wire line, it is advisable to substitute heavy braided nylon line, at least 100-pound-test, for the wire mentioned in Step 2. This is a safeguard against the effects of electrolysis.

For this type of deep-trolling, you can use either a rigged bait (ballyhoo, mullet, strip, feather-strip), or else a large lure, such as a spoon or feather.

FRESHWATER TROLLING RIGS

The two rigs shown are similar in purpose, although they differ in the type of sinker and baits shown. Both are widely used around the country, but particularly in the northern sectors, for trolling or deep-drifting. They are fine producers of many species that mostly stay deep, such as walleye, sauger and warm-weather trout. Both rigs incorporate a three-way sinker. The fishing line is tied to one eye, the dropline and sinker to another, and the leader with bait to the third. The latter often is only a piece of line clipped from the fishing line. The pencil sinker, shown with the jig-and-minnow, is not easily snagged and so is often used in larger rivers with rough bottom. The Dipsey sinker is a good one for many uses. It's shown here with an earthworm-and-flasher rig.

BREAKAWAY SINKERS

The obvious use of breakaway sinker rigs is to get your bait to the desired depth in situations which require so much weight that the sinker would be a disadvantage after a fish is hooked.

You can improvise a breakaway rig, using thread or light monofilament line, but the simplest and most effective method is to run a length of soft copper wire (such as you buy for rigging ballyhoo) twice through the eye of an egg sinker. This leaves some of the wire protruding from either end. Wrap one end lightly to the eye of your swivel; and wrap the other end around your leader with two or three wide spirals.

This will hold the sinker firmly enough in place so that you can drop it down. When a fish is hooked, the soft wire lets go usually on the first dash.

VERSATILE BOTTOM RIG

This is one of the most popular of bottom rigs, and can be used by

118

varying the size of hook and sinker in virtually every area of salt-water fishing—in bays, from bridges and piers, in the surf, and in deepwater partyboat angling. As you can see, it differs from the preceding pyramid sinker rig only in that a bank sinker (or other style) is used instead of the pyramid. Also, as the illustration shows, two or more three-way swivels may be incorporated into the leader for additional dropper lines with extra hooks.

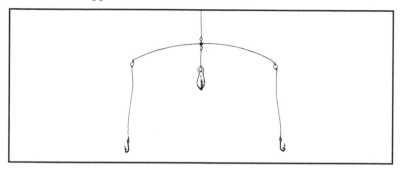

SPREADER BOTTOM RIG

Though used primarily for fluke and flounder fishing in bays, the spreader rig is a good one for fishing on any comparatively smooth bottom and for many types of fish.

While most anglers purchase them ready-rigged in tackle shops, it's not too difficult to fashion a spreader, using stiff, springy wire. Dropper lines for hooks and sinker are of monofilament. Your fishing line, of course, is tied to the swivel at the center of the spreader.

HEAVY BALL SINKER RIGS

Perfected in the San Francisco Bay area for getting baits down to striped bass when they are at depths which pretty much prohibit the usual rigs, heavy ball sinkers—sometimes weighing two pounds or more—are useful, too, in such specialties as plumbing extreme ocean depths for cod, snapper, grouper and tilefish.

One illustration shows the ball rigged to a three-way sinker as in preceding rigs with other types of weights. This would obviously require extremely heavy tackle and a lot of muscle to crank the ball

119

back up, either with or without a fish attached. It's best used with a motorized reel.

The detailed drawing shows a device popular in the Pacific northwest to release the ball once a fish is hooked, so the quarry can be fought on lighter tackle without the heavy weight. The sinker release is spring-loaded. You draw back the spring, insert the eye of the ball sinker into the aperture, and release the spring. When a bass or salmon hits, the spring is depressed and the sinker falls free. The sinker release is not used on a dropper line, but is simply tied into the leader by means of the swivels at each end.

THE MANY-PURPOSE STINGER RIG

Here's a rig that can be used effectively with both live and dead natural baits, even plastic worms, and is a snap to make. It's called the "Stinger" because the trailing hook nips short-striking fish, or those which usually clip a bait in the middle and avoid a single, forward-placed hook.

The rig can be made with either monofilament or wire leader, and in a variety of hook sizes for such diverse purposes as swordfishing with whole squid and 14/0 hooks, and rigging a sandworm to 1/0 hooks.

All the illustrations show the connection between front and rear hooks made with a swivel. This is advantageous, since it allows the rear hook to be turned at will in any direction necessary for affixing it to the particular bait; however, the swivel may be eliminated and the connection made directly to the eye of the forward hook.

In rigging, when you run the leader through the eye of the forward hook, run it through the eye of the swivel before tying or wrapping off. Then take a separate short length of leader, tie or wrap it to the other eye of the swivel, and then wrap the second hook to the end of it.

Many anglers routinely use the Stinger Rig with live baits, whether they be kite-flown, drifted, slow-trolled or free-lined.

When used with dead baits, such as strips, ballyhoo, cigar minnows or squid, the front hook is inserted at the front of the bait, in the bottom and out the top, and the second hook placed wherever it happens to reach. The front hook now serves the same purpose as the "pin" in a regular trolling-bait rig.

When grass is a problem, you would not wish to use a Stinger Rig for trolling—but it could be done. And the Stinger is the best of all rigs for drifting dead baits.

Float Rigs

How do you select the proper size and type of float? Follow these guidelines:

Cane-pole fishermen should use a very small float, or one of the slender designs (many still like the old turkey quill, of which there are numerous manufactured successors) so a bream or perch can take it under without feeling much resistance.

Larger floats are for bigger baits and, hopefully, bigger fish. The design is not actually too important. Just try to use the smallest size which will support the bait you're using. This is especially important with live baits. You don't want a float which can be easily pulled under, and kept under for long periods, by your bait. It can be difficult to tell when the strike comes.

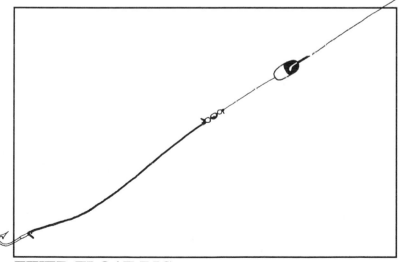

FIXED FLOAT RIG

This is the standard setup for fishing with a float. The rig remains basically the same, although it can be used with a wide array of floats—in various sizes and designs.

The float is placed at a predetermined depth, and fixed there so it will not move. The manner in which it is fixed, depends on the design of the float.

Many floats have a hollow center and a peg. You run the line through the center of the float and fix it in position by inserting the peg. Obviously, you must thread the float on your line before tying on your leader or hook.

Other floats have a spring-loaded clip. By simply pressing a button, you can affix or remove the float at will. These floats, however, tend to slip, and they also may weaken a light line when snapped directly to it.

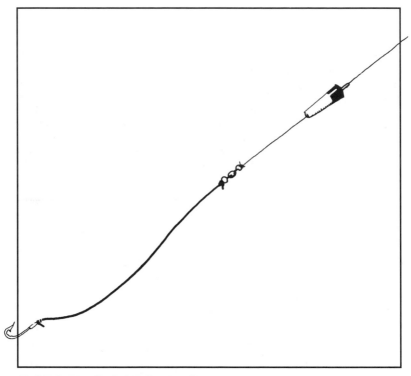

POPPING CORK RIG

This is the same as the fixed-float rig, the only difference being that you use a float which is specifically designed to pop the surface of the water when you twitch the tip of your rod.

Just like an ordinary float, the popping cork supports your bait at the desired depth, and signals a strike. But it also helps attract fish to your bait. Instead of letting the cork lie still, you pop it at frequent intervals (be sure to take up any slack line which results).

The noise is attractive to many predatory fish. The popping cork is most widely used for seatrout, but can be equally deadly on redfish, snook, jack and other species.

Popping corks are identifiable by their wide, scooped-out heads. They are available in weighted and unweighted models.

The unweighted model floats on its side when at rest. It pops well only if you're using a sinker between the cork and your bait.

The weighted model has a bit of lead molded inside of it, and so rides the surface head-up. Use the weighted one if you're fishing with no sinker.

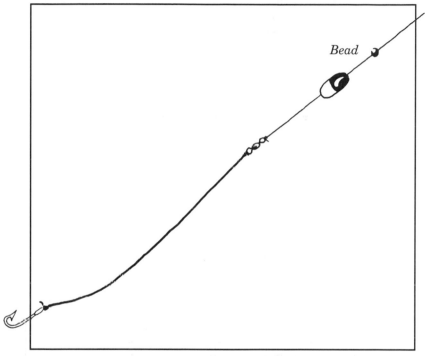

Bead

SLIDING OR CASTING FLOAT RIG

It can be awkward, or even impossible, to cast with a fixed float—especially if your float is several feet above the bait.

You want a float which slides right down to your swivel or sinker as you cast, yet stops at the desired depth after your bait hits the water.

To achieve this, you must use a sliding float in conjunction with a plastic, hollow bead.

First, tie a knot in your line at the point where you want the float to stop. Now thread the bead onto your line below the knot, then thread the float onto your line below the bead. Last, tie on your leader (or hook and sinker, if using no leader).

The hole in the bead is too small to permit passage of the knot, therefore the bead stops at the knot. And the bead, of course, stops the float. Beads can be purchased at tackle counters. If necessary, you could use a small button instead of the bead.

CAUTION: The knot you tie to stop the bead severely reduces the breaking strength of your line! Unless you're using quite heavy line, it pays to tie on a long length of monofilament shock leader, and to tie your stop-knot in that. Another option is to wrap a bit of tape around your line at the desired stopping point. A little thread wrapped tightly around the line will serve the same purpose. There also are tiny manufactured stopping devices of plastic, sold either alone or in a complete sliding-float kit.

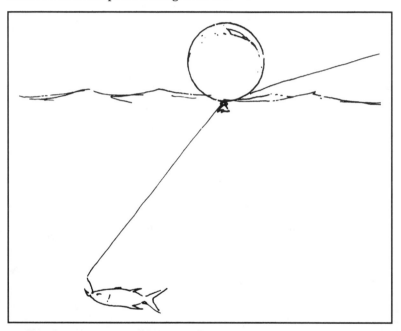

BREAKAWAY OR BALLOON FLOAT

One of the most versatile and easily carried of floats is an ordinary toy balloon. A package of balloons can be tucked away in a corner of your tackle box, out of the way until one is needed.

A balloon can be inflated to whatever size is needed to support your particular bait. Make a single knot in the balloon's lip to hold inflation, then tie the lip to your swivel or leader at the chosen depth, using a bit of light line for the purpose. The fight of a husky fish will burst the balloon, so that there is no added pressure on your rod as you tussle. Tie the balloon on tightly so that it does not become ocean litter after it breaks. Balloons make especially effective floats when you want to drift the bait far from boat, bridge or shore, as they are carried easily by wind and current.

Flyfishing Leaders

Most fly-fishing leaders are tapered leaders, built personally by the angler out of descendingly smaller diameters of monofilament leader material.

Tapered leaders cast much more efficiently than do level leaders. If properly matched to the fly (and if the mechanics of the cast are good) a tapered leader will always turn over neatly and deposit the fly at leader's length from the fly line.

When making tapered leaders, use the same brand of monofilament for all sections, since diameters may vary from brand to brand.

The sections may be tied together with either the Double Uni-Knot or Blood Knot. When a heavy tippet is used, it usually is tied on with the Albright Special, although the Uni or Surgeon's Knot can be used.

First step in making tapered leaders is to tie a short piece of 30-pound monofilament directly to the end of your fly line, using the Uni-Knot or Fast Nail Knot. Make a loop in the end of the short mono, using the Uni Loop or End Loop Knot. This loop serves as a convenient connector for your fly leaders, which are attached by interlocking loops.

The length of the mono "connector" can vary according to personal whim. Freshwater flyfishermen often keep it very short—just a few inches—and attach their entire pre-made or manufactured, knotless tapered leaders to it.

Saltwater anglers, on the other hand, are more inclined to make the connecting length of 30-pound mono from three to six feet long, thus treating it as the actual butt of their leaders. They make up the rest of the leader, including class tippet and heavy tippet (if any) as a unit, then attach it to the permanent butt.

24"	18"	12"	12"	6"	18
30-lb.	20-lb.	15-lb.	12-lb.	6-lb.	4-lb.

TROUT FLY LEADER

You can have a lot of fun fishing with this leader and small trout flies (dries, wets or nymphs) for panfish, such as bluegill, redbreast and crappie. Sometimes you can clobber bream with dry flies when they are reluctant to hit the usual popping bugs.

For trout fishing you can use this leader as your starter. But leaders for trout fishing vary greatly in length, strength and makeup, depending mainly on the character of the water being fished and the size and type of the flies used.

PANFISH-BASS LEADER

(Open water; small streamers or poppers)
This leader serves the same purposes as does the Level Leader to be described, but will prove much more satisfactory than the level in the long run, and should be chosen by anyone who wishes to become a practiced and proficient caster.

BASS OR SALTWATER LEADER

(Large streamers; large bugs)
This is the workhorse leader for inshore saltwater angling, as well as for bass fishing with big lures. Use it for trout, redfish, jack, many other types. For snook and small tarpon, you can add an additional one-foot Heavy Tippet of 40-pound-test monofilament. Tie this to the 12-pound material with the Albright Special or Surgeon's Knot.

For mackerel, barracuda or bluefish, you can add a one-foot Heavy Tippet of light wire cable, either plain or nylon-coated. Tie the cable to your 12-pound material with the Albright Special. Tie your fly to the cable with the Figure-Eight Knot.

HEAVY SALTWATER LEADER

This is the leader used for "big-game" fishing with the saltwater fly rod—giant tarpon, shark and various offshore species such as kingfish, amberjack, blackfin tuna, sailfish and other huskies. (If you're fishing specifically for dolphin, you can safely use the general-purpose saltwater leader described earlier.)

The makeup of this leader is simple, but you must prepare it with considerable time and care.

First, use the Uni-Knot or Fast Nail Knot to tie a leader butt of 30- or 40-pound-test monofilament to your fly line as described earlier. Six feet is the usual length.

Second, take a piece of 12-pound or 15-pound-test monofilament, six feet long, and make a double-line in both ends. Tie one of the double-line ends to the leader butt, using the Albright Special. Tie the other double-line end to your Heavy Tippet, again using the Albright Special.

After you get through doubling both ends of your light material, and tying them to butt and Heavy Tippet, your section of light material will measure somewhere around two feet long. If it comes out longer, you're O.K. Nor is there anything to worry about if it comes out slightly shorter than two feet. But if it comes out shorter than one foot, redo it.

Your Heavy Tippet should be one-foot, no longer. If tarpon fishing, make your Heavy Tippet of 100-pound-test monofilament. If offshore or shark fishing, make it of cable, or nylon-coated cable.

Tournament, club and International Game Fish Association rules all require that the light material ahead of the Heavy Tippet be no less than 12 inches long.

The same rules require that the Heavy Tippet itself be no longer than 12 inches, and this measurement must include the knots.

If your Heavy Tippet is of stout monofilament, tie it to your fly with the Two-Wrap Hangman's Knot. If using cable, tie on your fly with the Figure-Eight Knot.

LEVEL LEADER, NO-KNOT EYELET

Though trout fishermen would shudder, the most common fly leader used by southern freshwater anglers is simply a level length of monofilament, usually in 6-, 8- or 10-lb.-test, and seldom any longer than 6 or 7 feet.

Panfish and average-size bass are not very sophisticated, so the short level leader normally does an adequate job, and it casts well enough with the popper and plastic molded insects, which are the main lures used.

Simplest method of attaching the level leader is to tie or loop it to the short monofilament connecter described previously.

You might also use a manufactured No-Knot Eyelet, which is sold in most tackle stores. This is nothing more than a barbed straight pin with an eye in the end of it. Push the barbed pin carefully into the hollow core of your fly line. Tie your leader to the eye, using the Improved Clinch Knot.

The No-Knot Eyelet is very strong and not apt to fail in freshwater fishing, if carefully installed.

Chapter 7

Baits Rigs & Tackle

Freshwater Baits

LIVE BAITFISH

Live shiners, chubs and similar baitfish are the standard natural bait of bass fishermen everywhere. They can be purchased at bait shops and fishing camps, but the ones you buy are generally commercial hatchery baitfish and will probably be smaller and less hardy than those you catch yourself. But, of course, not everyone has the time or inclination to catch his own shiners.

Avid seekers of trophy-size bass prefer to catch their own native shiners, using cane pole, light bobber and No. 10 hook with bread balls for bait. Liberal chumming with watered bread helps attract shiners to the bait.

Native shiners often run six or eight inches in length, and some-

Sucker for muskie, hooked through nose.

times nine or 10 inches. They don't come too big to suit bass anglers who seek huge largemouths.

Naturally, more action can be expected with the small shiners, and some very big bass often hit little baits.

Smaller, bait-store shiners should be used with about a 3/0 hook. With big native shiners, tie on at least a 5/0 hook, and don't be afraid to use hooks as large as 8/0—preferably in a bronzed freshwater pattern.

When you're using a float rig, it's usually best to hook the shiner lightly through the dorsal surface. However, when drift-fishing or slow trolling (with a bobber or without) you'll get more natural swimming action by hooking through both lips.

In weedy areas, a large weedless hook can be used, and the lip hookup is best for this.

LIVE BREAM

Small bream (usually bluegill, but other species of sunfish can be used too) make excellent baits for bass in states where legal.

As with shiners, larger bream are apt to lure bigger bass.

Hook bream exactly the same as described for shiners.

There's absolutely no doubt that shiners are much preferred for bass bait by fishermen in general. However, quite a few specialists use bream by choice. Note too that there will be times when shiners are scarce, but a few bream can almost always be taken by fishing with worms or bread balls.

131

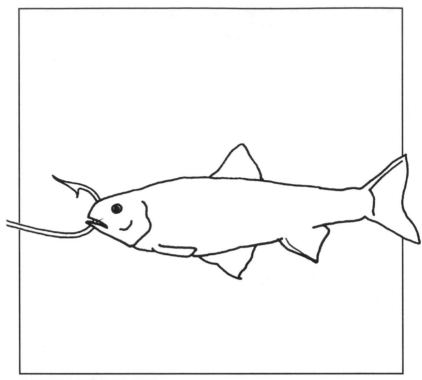

LIVE MINNOWS

The great majority of small live minnows used in freshwater fishing are dunked by anglers seeking crappie. But as the devout sweetwater fisherman has learned long ago, minnows will take just about anything that swims—yellow perch and walleye, rock bass and warmouth, pickerel, white bass, striped bass, black bass, even catfish.

Occasionally a crappie fisherman will miss out on his primary target, but return to dock with a nifty string of bluegills or warmouth—all caught on minnows. And stories are legion concerning crappie fishermen who find an 8- or 10-pound bass wallowing around on the end of their cane-pole line.

Because of their flimsy size, it's difficult to hook minnows through the back without doing them serious injury—even with very light-wire hooks. Therefore, the most common hookup for small minnows is through both lips.

Use only the tiniest of split-shot sinkers when fishing a minnow. This is a fragile bait that can't carry around much weight.

Should you run out of live minnows, dead ones can often be used with success if you hook them through the lips, then twitch your pole or rod to make the dead bait move through the water.

LIVE FROGS

Everybody knows that live frogs make great bait for bass. Members of the pike family are especially fond of frogs as well. Still, frogs are not used too often anymore because of the difficulty in procuring and handling them in fishable quantity. Some anglers go to frogs as a last resort—only when other baits aren't working. Then they chase down a frog or two. More often than not, the frog produces action.

The frog can be hooked lightly through one leg. Frog skin is tough and the hook seldom pulls out. If presented with no sinker or other terminal tackle, the leg-hooked frog really kicks up a commotion and attracts fish. Another common hookup is through both lips, as with a shiner or minnow.

In a clear-water situation, where perhaps you can see bass—and they can see you—a leg-hooked frog, presented on a light monofilament line with no other terminal tackle, will draw a strike when all else fails.

Sometimes you'll encounter a great number of very small frogs on the bank of a lake or river. These are easily caught and make fine bait for panfish. Use No. 8 hooks on pole or light spinning tackle, and hook the frogs in exactly the same way as already described.

CRAWFISH

Many river and creek fishermen swear by crawfish—the larger specimens for bass—particularly smallmouth—and the smaller ones for panfish. Of course lake fish will eat crawfish too, but this bait is at its best when allowed to drift along with the current of a stream.

The easiest way to get crawfish is with a light and dipnet at night along the shallow edges of a stream. They roam and feed at night and are easily spotted with a light. You can get some in the daytime by turning over rocks and limbs in shallow water or small pools. Watch out for the pinchers—they nip painfully, but do no serious damage to your fingers.

Like live shrimp in salt water, crawfish can be hooked lightly through the top of their hard forward shell (carapace). Most anglers, however, prefer to hook them through the tail as shown in the illustration. This helps a lot in keeping the crawfish from backing under a rock or root.

Toss the crawfish upstream, using a sinker just heavy enough to get you down near bottom. Let the current carry the bait downstream.

You may remove the claws without harming the bait's appeal but folks who use crawfish often quickly learn to handle them and hook them up without getting pinched.

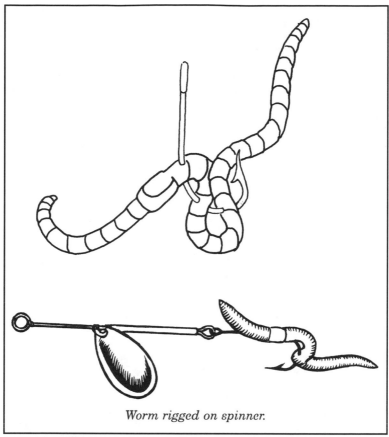

Worm rigged on spinner.

EARTHWORMS

From tiny red wigglers to huge "pond worms" and night crawlers, earthworms have been used by more freshwater fishermen than all other baits combined. And so it probably always will be, because worms just catch fish.

There are many ways of hooking worms, but the one illustrated is very productive and very commonly used. Hook once through the center section, then turn the hook and go through the center section once more. If the bend of your hook is large enough, go through a third time.

This leaves both long ends of the worm free to wave around in the water—and the action attracts trout, bass and those big bream just as much as whatever smell and taste appeal the worm might have. Seldom do you miss hooking a fat panfish with this hookup. Little ones will sometimes grab the end of a free-waving worm, but you don't want those anyway.

Kids, of course, often use a small piece of worm and thread it on

135

the hook. That's because they don't want to miss those nibbling little fish. And if you wish to catch some little fellows for bait, then you can thread a tiny piece of worm too.

If you're going for catfish or carp, you'll want to use a "gob" of worms. Probably you'll select a No. 1 or 1/0 hook. Start with one worm and hook it two or three times through the middle as described above—but then hook it two or three more times. Now push the worm all the way up the hook shank to the eye of the hook; take another worm and hook it several times in the same fashion, then push it close against the first worm.

Use as many worms as it takes to cover the hook completely, from barb to eye, with just what the name implies—a real gob of worms. Naturally, the number of worms needed to make a gob will vary according to the size of your worms and the size of your hook.

PROCURING WORMS

There are many ways to get worms—the easiest way being to go into a bait store and buy them.

If you prefer to dig your worms, look for them in soft, moist earth. Generally they can be found near a spring or well, or near an outside faucet where the ground stays wet. If no water source is nearby, you can tell good worm territory by examining the ground for the tiny hills of dirt that worms leave on the surface.

Most lawns in good condition are excellent worm territory but, naturally you don't go around digging up your lawn—or a lawn belonging to anyone else, for that matter. What you CAN do is search the lawn at night with a flashlight, especially after a rain. Worms often come out at night and can simply be picked up.

Another way to get worms from a lawn (or from other good worm territory) without having to dig is by "grunting" them. Your leg isn't being pulled. Grunting works!

Drive a wooden stake into the ground, leaving a couple inches exposed above the surface. Rub the top of the stake with a large rasp, or any other rough metallic object that gives a good grating effect. Vibrations set off by this grunting drive the worms (if any are within range of the vibrations) to the surface.

CRICKETS AND GRASSHOPPERS

While crickets are selected as bait far more often than grasshoppers—for the simple reason they are widely sold in bait shops, while grasshoppers are not—both insects are effective fish producers, and both are fished in the same way.

Both should be hooked through the thorax, which is the forward, crusty half of the body. The rear portion is soft and tears loose easily. You can run the hook in one side of the thorax and out the other, or else (as in the illustration), run the hook through from top to bottom.

There is no way to hook a cricket or grasshopper so that it will stay alive for any great length of time. But when hooked through the thorax they stay alive for a reasonable period. Besides, when fished beneath the surface, a dead cricket is just as effective as a live one. Many people do all their fishing with crickets below the surface—using a small hook, split shot, and a very light cork or bobber.

An excellent method, particularly in rivers and creeks, is to present the cricket with no terminal tackle of any kind except, of course, the light hook. It will float along, kicking at the surface for a while, then will begin to settle slowly. Big bream seldom can resist such a natural presentation, and they may strike anywhere from the surface to the deepest depth the unweighted cricket can attain.

Crickets and grasshoppers are widely considered to be the leading stream baits for panfish, but they do work in lakes and ponds too.

As mentioned, crickets are sold at most bait stores. You can catch your own—but don't depend on catching enough bait the same day you plan to fish. It's much better to set aside an afternoon, catch your crickets, and keep them until the day of your trip. They will stay healthy and happy indefinitely in any mesh box or cage, with a few potato peelings for them to feed on.

Commercially-raised crickets, the kind sold at bait counters, are light in color and referred to as gray crickets. The ones you catch in the wild will be somewhat larger and much darker, deep brown or black. Regardless of color or species or size, they all seem to produce equally well.

Look for wild crickets in pastures or open fields, especially those liberally strewn with fallen limbs and other things the crickets can hide under. Turn over limbs, debris—anything crickets might hide under. They almost always stay hidden during the day.

While you hunt for crickets, you'll kick up grasshoppers from grass and low brush. Catch them if you like, for they make just as good an offering to the fish. However, catching grasshoppers requires more effort, since they often must be chased. Crickets don't move nearly as fast, or in such long hops.

Certain lighted areas attract crickets at night. Try, for instance, the parking lot of a lighted shopping center after closing hours (be careful that the security guards or police don't call for the paddy-wagon). You can make the rounds of many lighted areas at the edge of town, near open fields or lots, and probably discover one or more places where crickets congregate. If you do, you'll have a dependable source of bait.

Insect Larvae

A great many common insects undergo a metamorphosis: that is, a change from one form to another during their life cycle. These insects begin life in a worm-like stage, when they are called larvae. Next, they go into a dormant or pupal stage, during which they change into adult form. Well-known examples of larvae are the various caterpillars, which become moths and butterflies, and grubs, which become beetles.

So much for the lesson on entomology. The point for fishermen is that many, many types of larvae make excellent bait. Some larvae are commonly sold in bait shops; others are not, but can easily be obtained in the right place and right season.

CATERPILLARS

Fishermen generally refer to fish-bait caterpillars as "worms," and identify the various species to their satisfaction simply by tacking on the name of the tree on which the worm is found: for instance, "catalpa worm," "oak worm," "pecan worm," "camphor worm."

The catalpa worm is by far the most widely popular of bait caterpillars, and not a few fishermen keep catalpa trees for the sole purpose of raising a yearly crop of good bream bait. When small, catalpa worms are used whole on the hook. When they get big (and they do get real big) they are often broken in half, and sometimes turned inside-out before going on the hook—not a procedure for the queasy, obviously, but darn good bait for both big panfish and catfish. Oak worms appear in great number on small oak trees, notably the blackjack oak, in early fall. Camphor trees get their crop of bait worms in late summer. Of course, these seasons vary slightly from area to area.

Actually, just about any kind of caterpillar makes good bait.

There are exceptions, of course, and they can be painful exceptions. Shy away from stinging kinds, such as the saddle-back caterpillar, and all species which are covered with thick fuzz. Some very good bait species, however (including the oak worm and pecan worm), have small but soft bristles which are harmless.

When small caterpillars are used for bait, they can be threaded on your hook as the illustration shows. Larger ones should be hooked once or twice at the tail end. If the skin of the caterpillar is tough, bring the point and barb of the hook outside the skin for easier hooking of the fish.

GRUBS

Most insect larvae referred to as "grubs" or "grub worms" are white or yellowish in color and have prominent hard heads with visible mandibles or pinchers. The majority are larvae of various beetles, and are found either in soft ground or under the bark of trees—usually dead trees but sometimes, as in the case of pine, in living trees as well.

Those aforementioned pinchers can indeed pinch. But you can safely use the bait simply by keeping your fingers away from the business end. One type of grub is called "sawyer." You'll sometimes find a rotting pine log in the woods so full of sawyers that you can hear them grinding away from several feet. Their noise sounds like sawing, hence the name. Sawyers are excellent bream baits.

Commercially-sold grubs include those called meal worms and golden grubs.

Most grubs are small and should be threaded onto the hook as in the illustration.

BONNET WORMS

Actually, bonnet worms are caterpillars and should perhaps have been included in that category. But most fishermen don't think of them as caterpillars because of their habitat. They are found in the stems of bonnets, or lily pads, right out in the water. Look for pads which have a visible hole in the stem, right in the center of the pad. Pull up the stem and slit it carefully, and you'll find the worm (unless, of course, it has attained adulthood and departed). An awful lot of bream fishermen say bonnet worms are the very best baits of all.

MAGGOTS

The larval baits called "maggots" represent a variety of insect species, none of which is likely to be the common house fly. That should make you feel better! Baits called "sand maggots" are locally procured and sold at many bait stores in the south. In addition, various small maggots may be bought in tins in local bait shops and from mail-order houses. Some of these are even dyed in various colors to appeal to style-conscious fish. The name "maggot" has an unappetizing connotation, but the creatures used for bait are far less repulsive than their name suggests. They are, in fact, cleaner to handle and easier to use than most other larval baits.

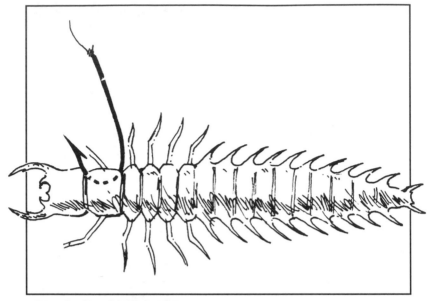

HELLGRAMMITE

Hellgrammites are the larvae of dobson flies and rank among the best all-around baits for river fishing, inasmuch as they are greedily snapped up by largemouth and smallmouth bass, trout and a variety of panfish. They are tough to corral, but can be taken by overturning logs and driftwood in slow-moving sections of streams. Careful—they can nip painfully. They are best fished by hooking once through the segmented body near the tail, then bumping them with the current along the bottom. In some areas of the south, hellgrammites are called "Gator fleas," and a few folks still believe that the hellgrammite goes out and catches the fish, instead of vice versa. This myth developed because the hellgrammite defensively grabs hold of any fish that bites it, and occasionally a panfish will be landed even when the hook pulls free—because the "flea" hangs on.

GRASS SHRIMP

Small shrimp inhabit many fresh waters and are commonly called "grass shrimp." Many bait stores carry them, and if you know your waters you can dipnet or seine them from grassy areas.

Grass shrimp are small and it often takes two or three to make a suitable bait, even on a small bream hook. The illustration is deliberately magnified in effect, so you can see how several grass shrimp should be hooked at one time. Of course, any suitably large specimen you might find in your bait supply can be used singly.

Like saltwater shrimp, grass shrimp can be kept alive for a long time without being kept in water. They should be kept in a cold container, moist, but protected from actually sitting in water. You can keep them in a can, or a waxed paper cup which, in turn, is placed in your portable ice chest.

If you don't carry an ice chest, keep them in a can on a bed of moist weed, cloth or newspaper.

SALMON EGGS

Salmon eggs are a natural food of trout and are taken avidly by many other fish—including varieties which never even saw a salmon egg except for the processed kind sold in jars as bait. The eggs can be fished singly or in globs. A single egg obviously requires a very small hook and a careful hookup, such as that illustrated above. The egg should be allowed to drift as naturally as possible along bottom in imitation of an egg swept along by the current. Globs of eggs must be aided in staying on the hook. If you use a snelled hook, then push the snell knot down on the shank, a bulge of line is formed. A portion of the egg cluster can be inserted under this bulge, which is then tightened. Or additional line can be pulled from above the knot and looped around the hook and the cluster. Another method is to tie the eggs in very fine netting. Artificial salmon eggs often work very well, and when fish are really gorging on eggs, they readily hit small spinners and other artificials which are colored orange or deep pink.

CATFISH BAITS

Since catfish will bite just about anything, it's surprising to see how many catfishermen go to the trouble of preparing special baits made out of blood, or smelly cheese or other unsavory substances. But they do catch catfish, and so you can't argue with them.

Many catfish enthusiasts keep their frying pans well supplied and never use any bait other than plain old earthworms (see the category headed "Earthworms" for instructions on making a catfish worm-gob).

Cats also will happily bite any of the other bream baits mentioned in these pages, and channel cats seem to show a special fondness for fat caterpillars.

Perhaps one reason so many catfishermen use special baits is that they don't want to be bothered by bream—especially the small bait-stealers.

If you want bait particularly for catfish, but don't wish to go in for special preparations, you can hardly do better than to slice up some beef or pork liver. For that matter, any kind of liver works.

Another popular catfish bait is a piece of frozen shrimp. Chunks of cut bait, from any kind of fish you can get your hands on, are also fine catfish producers, and are probably the most-used baits on trot lines.

144

Chapter 8

Baits Rigs & Tackle

Saltwater Baits

LIVE FISH

Every coastal area has its popular types of live baitfish-anchovy, menhaden (mossbunker), mullet, sardine, shiner, spot, grunt, pinfish, cigar minnow, chub, mummichog, blue runner and goggle-eye, to name just a few examples.

When you get right down to it, virtually any small fish of appropriate size can be used for live bait.

A live catfish, for instance, makes an excellent bait for cobia, tarpon and snook. And stomach samples of deep sea fishes—from billfish to bottom feeders—prove they regularly eat such oddities as porcupine fish, trunk fish, file fish, etc.

The whole point is this: use the popular baits whenever possible—after all, they're proven. But if you can't get the desired species of baitfish, don't hesitate to put out any small fish you can

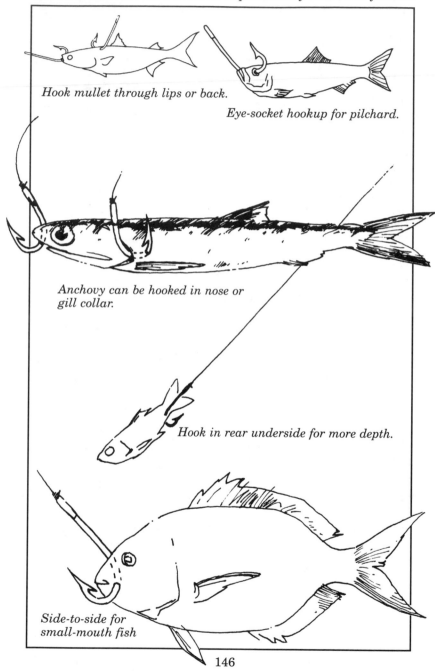

Hook mullet through lips or back.

Eye-socket hookup for pilchard.

Anchovy can be hooked in nose or gill collar.

Hook in rear underside for more depth.

Side-to-side for small-mouth fish

come up with. Chances are, the fish care less than you do.

Placement of the hook in a live bait is important and can vary according to the species of baitfish and how you want it to act.

The two hook positions in the mullet illustrated above are common ones, used with many different types of fish. One hookup is through either both lips or through the upper lip only; the other through the back.

Use the lip hookup when slow-trolling, or any time when boat motion or current would tend to pull a back-hooked bait through the water sideways, or in an unnatural way.

Some anglers feel that small-mouthed baitfish, such as mullet or pinfish, should not be hooked through both lips for fear of impairing "breathing" ability and shortening bait life. Mullet often are hooked by inserting the hook point into the mouth, then upward through the top lip only. Bait such as pinfish or spot may be hooked from side to side just back of the jaws.

The back hookup generally is a better placement, since a striking fish is more apt to get the hook on its initial hit. So hook through the back whenever it allows you to present the bait so that it swims in a free and natural manner. Placing the hook forward in the back tends to keep the bait nearer the surface. Hook it toward the tail if you want it to swim downward.

Placing the hook just behind the anal fin, on the bottom of the baitfish, above, is best of all for trying to urge the bait down deep.

Hook placement in other portions of the bait's anatomy may be necessary because of the nature of the species. Shown above are the two hookups most commonly used by California anglers with live anchovies. The hook can be stuck through either the tough "nose" of the fish, or through the bony "collar" just aft of the gills.

Similarly, some of the many baitfish species that are variously labeled sardines, pilchards, white bait, etc., may be too soft-fleshed to permit a reliable hookup through either the dorsal or the lips. A solution, as illustrated, is to run the hook through the eye socket, just above the eye.

CATCHING AND FISHING LIVE BALLYHOO

Ballyhoo, also called balao or halfbeak, has been employed for many years by ocean anglers as a standard dead bait. It is rigged whole for trolling, or is cut into strips and chunks.

In recent years, anglers have discovered that ballyhoo also make one of the premier live baits for many varieties of offshore game fish, and are well worth the effort it takes to catch them. Live ballyhoo are never found in bait shops because of the difficulty of keeping them alive and in good condition for any length of time.

While live-ballyhoo angling was developed in the Florida Keys and is still centered there, opportunities to catch and use these splendid baitfish exist in many warm waters of the world—in the Bahamas, throughout the Caribbean and tropical Latin America, and in many areas of the Pacific.

When disturbed, ballyhoo skitter across the surface of the water somewhat like flying fish, and this is how anglers often find them. Once skittering ballyhoo are located, the boat is anchored and a chum line begun. Ballyhoo respond readily to standard chums made from ground fish, and can also be chummed up with oatmeal or cracker crumbs. They stay at the top and can be spotted dimpling the surface of the water in the chum line. Once ballyhoo are near the boat, they can be caught by using very light line—no more than 10-pound test—to which is tied a No. 10 or No. 12 hair hook. The bait can be a tiny bit of cut fish or cut shrimp. Though an oldfashioned fishing pole makes the best ballyhoo-angling tool, few salty anglers are so equipped and most use light spinning rods (some do, however, keep telescoping glass poles aboard just for ballyhoo).

Regardless of what tackle is used, the bait must be drifted at the surface or just under it, and kept in sight by the angler so he can see the ballyhoo take the bait. Otherwise, he would not catch any, as ballyhoo do not deliver smashing strikes.

Even though it might be possible to catch a lot of them, you should resist the impulse to load up the baitwell with more than it can accommodate. Large, well-aerated wells on cabin cruisers—especially if their shape is round—can keep two or three dozen baits alive over a fishing day, but wells on small boats often cannot effectively keep more than a half-dozen.

When trolled for sailfish and other offshore species, a live ballyhoo should be pulled at just above idle speed. This is probably the slowest pace used for any bait. Ballyhoo also can be free-drifted or used on a kite. For that matter, many good fish are caught simply by drifting out a live ballyhoo on the very spot where you are catching the bait.

Ballyhoo belong to the group of fishes known as halfbeaks, and when you get your first close look at one it will surprise you to see that the "bill" is not an extension of the upper jaw but of the lower one. This curious physiognomy is the key to how you hook them.

Insert the hook into the mouth, point upward, and bring it out the top of the upper jaw. A small hook should be used, as a large one not only would tear out easily but would also diminish the action of the bait. Usual sizes are from 3/0 to 7/0, and in a rather light-wire hook, or a short-shank live-bait hook. The hook shank can be secured to the beak with a bit of copper wire.

Many anglers use an alternate system of mouth-hooking. They

thread a piece of ordinary soda straw, maybe three inches long, onto the leader. They affix the hook downward through the lower jaw at the base of the bill, then slide the soda straw forward, over both the bill and the hook shank, thus securing it firmly.

A mouth hookup is the proper one for trolling, drifting, or for free-lining the ballyhoo in a current.

For kite-fishing, or for free-lining when current is not a problem, you may prefer to hook the ballyhoo through the dorsal surface near the midway point—taking care not to injure the spine.

RIGGING LIVE BONITO

A live bonito probably is the best of all baits for offshore trolling—small ones measuring a foot or less for sailfish and other relatively small offshore species with tackle up to 50-pound-test; and larger live bonito for big marlin on heavy tackle.

Since live bonito of any size are often hard to procure, and because they don't live long in the average bait well, they usually are picked up individually on a small trolling feather and put to use at once.

In the interest of speed (when you aren't prepared in advance for a better hookup) hook your bonito through the lips and troll it slowly.

Properly, however, you should have a bait-needle ready, threaded with about 6 inches of nylon or Dacron line (20- or 30-pound-test). When the bonito comes aboard, have someone hold him firmly but gently with wet gloves, while you run the needle through the eye socket at about the 10 o'clock position. Remove the needle and quickly tie the ends of the line together to make a circle. The Surgeon's Knot, or simply a couple of overhand knots will do the job.

Now tie the circle of line in the middle, thus forming a figure-eight. Take the free end of the figure-eight and hitch it two or three times around your hook. The bait is ready to use.

If you're a serious marlin fisherman and want the best possible live bonito rig, get some preformed figure-eights made of brass. These are sold in most hardware stores (they're used as connectors for light chain).

To rig the metal figure-eight, use the bait-needle as before to thread a line through the bonito's eye socket. Tie the line tightly to one loop of the figure-eight, as close as possible to the bonito's head. Now you simply fix the other loop of the figure-eight over the bend of your hook. Obviously, when buying the figure-eights, you must be sure they are large enough to fit your chosen hook.

The metal figure-eight, because it is not bound tightly to the hook, allows the bait much more freedom of action. With this rig you can troll at your normal speed for dead-bait trolling instead of having to slow down—thus you do not have to retire your dead-bait lines when adding a live bonito to your spread.

Speed is of the utmost importance in getting a live bonito on the hook and back in the water. You should be able to rig in a few seconds, so practice rigging on dead baits until you can do the job efficiently but quickly.

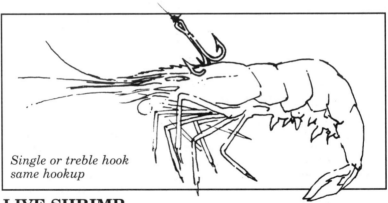

Single or treble hook same hookup

LIVE SHRIMP

King of live baits for coastal fishing is the live shrimp. It will take anything from bottom feeders to tarpon and king mackerel.

Some anglers hook their shrimp lightly through the tail, but these are the two most common hookups:

1. Through the head, either by running the point of your hook lightly under the horny ridge atop the head (as above), or from top to bottom through the head, taking care to keep the hook in front of the dark spot inside the head (as shown in the shrimp-and-jig rig, described later).

2. Threading. Insert the point on the underside of the tail, then work it the full length of the tail section and out in back of the head.

System No. 1 allows the shrimp to move about freely. It is a good choice in situations where fish are extremely selective. The obvious disadvantage is that the hookup is flimsy. This means the bait is

150

easily stolen by smaller fish. Still, you must use this hookup whenever it appears the fish are insisting on the most natural, free-swimming presentation.

System No. 2—the threaded shrimp—is considerably more durable and equally productive in many kinds of fishing, such as when letting the shrimp lie on bottom. A lot of anglers use the flimsy head hookup when it really isn't necessary, thus wasting much expensive bait.

The threaded shrimp is entirely satisfactory for trout, redfish, bonefish, most snapper, grouper and many other species. Your shrimp should be threaded when using the popping cork (which see), because a head-hooked shrimp can be popped right off your hook. And, of course, the threaded bait is given plenty of action by your popping motions.

If a threaded shrimp works so well, why not use dead bait instead of live? Well, sometimes you can and get good results. But experienced anglers know that the more desirable species of fish somehow prefer a shrimp with live appearance, smell and taste, over a dead shrimp—even though the live one may not be moving about.

LIVE SHRIMP WITH JIGHEAD

Although many rigs incorporate artificial lures with dead, cut or rigged baits, not many combine live bait with artificials. The reason is obvious: artificial lures must be given motion by the angler in order to produce efficiently; live baits are generally left to provide their own movement, which should be as natural and unfettered as possible.

A certain few lure-live bait combinations, however, rank among the best of all fish-catchers. In salt water one of the leading examples is the marriage of a live shrimp and a leaded jig-head. One such head, the Troll Rite is marketed for just that purpose, but any leaded hook—whether salvaged from an old jig or purchased new—will serve as well.

Since this rig does its best work right smack on bottom, the weight of the jig may have to be juggled in order to obtain the desired depth. In coastal shallows, one-quarter ounce is the usual size, but a half-ounce often is needed, and sometimes a head weighing up to an ounce is used in deeper channels and passes, particularly when there is strong current.

Start the point of the hook under the shrimp's "chin" and bring it out the top of the head—taking care to avoid damaging the dark spot which is visible in the head of the shrimp.

Make a long cast either directly upcurrent, or upcurrent and quartering away. Be sure to allow the rig to sink all the way to bottom, then retrieve just fast enough to keep a tight line as it works down with the current. You will, however, have to help keep it moving at times by very softly lifting the rodtip a few inches and increasing your retrieve rate just slightly. With a bit of practice you develop a "feel" for crawling the gadget along bottom, and your lifts of the rod at intervals impart a natural up-and-down movement to the shrimp.

The Troll Rite also can be fished effectively where there is no current at all. In this case, simply make a long cast and, again, allow it to sink to bottom. Holding your rodtip right at the surface, turn your reel crank v-e-r-y slowly—more slowly, probably, than you have ever retrieved a lure in your life, even an artificial worm. Just a bit too much speed and the shrimp will go off keel and begin to turn. With a creeping pace, however, the shrimp will move upright and naturally, with its legs churning.

No need even to attempt listing the species of fish a jig-live shrimp combination attracts, since just about everything from large game fish to panfish (and, unfortunately, trash fish as well) love a slow-moving shrimp.

LIVE BAITFISH WITH JIGHEAD

In certain situations, the combination of a jig head with a live baitfish can also be used with effect. One such instance would be for "hanging" a baitfish deep in a moving current where game fish are foraging. Hook the bait through both lips, let it out in the current, and when the desired position is reached, lock the reel and then either hold it or place it in a rod holder.

Hooked upward through the lips, the baitfish will hold a pretty normal attitude, facing into the current like a free-swimming fish, and the jig head helps hold it upright most of the time.

The bait will do a bit of swinging, and even turn on its side at times, but this is all to the good, since a sudden flash or a quick movement that simulates a fish in distress often touches off a strike.

Another application of the jig-baitfish rig is to cover a desired path of retrieve, as with the jig-shrimp. Cast the bait out and bring it back at a creeping pace over the selected course. Remember that a fast, or even a medium, retrieve rate will probably cause the baitfish to twist.

KEEPING LIVE SHRIMP

A good livewell, with recirculating water or an aerator, is the most satisfactory repository for live shrimp.

Bait buckets with a removable perforated inner container work quite well. The inner container is kept on a line in the water while you're fishing. If you move, the bucket is filled with water and the container placed inside. But if you have a long distance to travel, be sure to change the water frequently.

An even better bucket is the one-piece type that provides all the advantages of the traditional two-piece. It has a solid bottom and perforated top. It lies on its side when in the water, thus permitting good flow, but retains water in the bottom when hauled up to deck or dock.

THE ICING SYSTEM is an excellent one and will keep shrimp alive, without water, for several hours—even for a full day or more if you're careful. Here's how it works:

The shrimp must be transferred directly from the dealer's well into a water-tight container—a large waxed paper cup, an old coffee can, or even a plastic bag. This container then must be kept very cold, in an ice chest, but the shrimp must, at all times, be kept from coming in contact with water from the melting ice.

The colder you keep your ice chest, the longer your shrimp stay alive. It's best to have a separate small ice chest just for your shrimp. General-purpose ice chests are opened too frequently for drinks, etc., and this brings up the inside temperature.

CAUTION: Don't transport your shrimp on ice, then remove them and place them in a live well. If you use the icing method, stick with it all the way.

LIVE BLUE CRAB

The live blue crab is a standard bait for permit fishing and for tarpon in deep channels. It also works well on many other fish, including redfish, drum, snapper, grouper, and snook.

"Dollar crabs"—that is, crabs approximating the size of a silver dollar—are the choice for both permit and tarpon. Tarpon will take larger crabs, but seem to favor the smaller ones.

Large live crabs make an excellent bait for deep bottom fishing for snapper and grouper. Let's say you've been fishing a deep hole or wreck where you can't avoid hooking amberjack every time you drop a live fish, or even a strip. You want to get past the amberjacks and try for a big snapper or grouper. The live crab is your solution. Amberjack won't touch it, yet the bottom fish love it.

No matter what size crab you use, remove the claws (for your personal safety), and hook as shown through the tip of the shell.

Crabs are easy to keep alive, either in a bait well or simply in a cool, damp place—such as a wet burlap sack.

SAND FLEA

The sand flea is a specialized bait, used almost exclusively by surf and ocean-pier fishermen for pompano. It will take other surf species as well, but is unsurpassed as a pompano bait along beaches.

Sand fleas (not really fleas, but crustaceans) are sold at many beachside tackle shops, or they can be caught by the angler. Look for them at the edge of the surf where waves roll up on the sand, and then recede. As the wave recedes, look for V-shaped wakes in the soupy sand, made by the protruding antennae of the sand flea.

You must immediately scoop them out by digging under the "V" with your hand, to bring up a handful of sand which, you hope, has the sand flea in the middle of it.

Surf regulars build a special scoop, which can be compared to a shovel with a wire-mesh bottom. They spot the antennae; dig out a big scoopful of sand; then let the sand filter through the mesh, leaving the fleas. Sometimes they get several baits at one scoop.

Hook the sand flea as shown in the illustration—once through from bottom to top.

FIDDLER CRAB

A traditional bait for sheepshead, the fiddler crab can be found almost everywhere in tidal areas (though abundance varies with season). Besides sheepshead, fiddlers take snapper, redfish, grouper, drum—even an occasional snook.

You may find fiddlers on sandy shores, mud flats, or among mangrove roots. Sometimes they're in bunches that resemble waves moving across the sand. Unless they reach their holes, they are easy to chase and capture by hand.

Do not fear the one overgrown claw which gives the fiddler its name. Though it looks wicked indeed, it has little strength. The pinch of a fiddler crab can't break the skin, or even cause enough pain to make you say "Ouch."

To bait up with a fiddler, run your hook in at the base of any leg, and out anywhere under the shell.

LIVE CRAWFISH

A live crawfish of legal size makes a mouthful of bait indeed. As you can guess, it's used only for big fish—giant cubera snapper mainly, along the lower east coast of Florida and the Keys. Occasionally, the live crawfish is chosen as a bait for jewfish or big grouper.

Baby crawfish would be good bait for many fish, but it is unlawful to use them in Florida waters.

Obviously, the crawfish referred to is the saltwater variety, also called Florida lobster.

The double-hook rig shown here is the most satisfactory for cubera snapper fishing. Use two heavy-duty hooks, at least 9/0 and usually larger, and wire them together with cable and sleeves (see

155

the section on wire wraps for instructions on securing the cable). The hooks are about four or five inches apart.

As the illustration shows, the upper hook goes between the "horns" of the crawfish. The lower one is inserted into the soft underside of the tail section, and out again.

Always handle live crawfish with gloves.

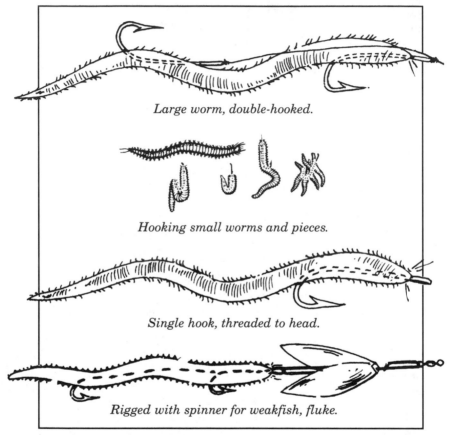

Large worm, double-hooked.

Hooking small worms and pieces.

Single hook, threaded to head.

Rigged with spinner for weakfish, fluke.

MARINE WORMS

Soft-bodied marine worms (sandworms, bloodworms, clamworms, etc.) are excellent all-around baits and one of the most popular along the Middle and North Atlantic coasts. As shown in the small illustrations, chunks, pieces or whole tiny worms can be used for panfish—perhaps even several tiny worms on a single hook. Larger worms, rigged to a single or double hook, or behind a spinner, make excellent trolling, drifting or still-fishing baits for larger prey, such as weakfish, striped bass and flounder. An easy double hookup is accomplished with the Stinger Rig, shown in Chapter 3.

Rigged Trolling Baits

BALLYHOO (BALAO)

Once you learn it—and it doesn't take long—the ballyhoo is the simplest and fastest-to-rig of all offshore trolling baits. This, combined with the fact that it is an excellent producer of everything from marlin to mackerel, makes the ballyhoo top choice among both professional and private skippers.

The rigged ballyhoo is most often trolled at the surface, skipping across the waves. But it is rigged in exactly the same fashion for deep-trolling with a sinker, or for drift-fishing, either with a free line or with a sinker.

First step in making a ballyhoo rig is to leave a "pin" in your wire leader after wrapping on the hook. Study the illustration. The pin should be at right angles to the leader, and pointing in the opposite direction from the hook. The leader wrap, of course, is made with the Haywire twist as usual. Only difference is that you do not break off the excess wire; you cut off the excess, leaving enough for the pin.

Now take a piece of copper wire (which you buy in precut lengths

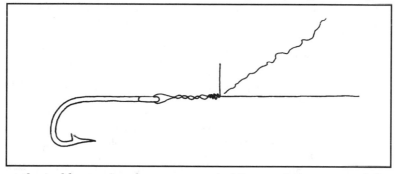

at the tackle store) and wrap one end of it several times around the leader wire at the base of the pin.

If ballyhoo is frozen, thaw it in a bucket of sea water before rigging.

Take the ballyhoo in your hands and bend it back and forth several times. This breaks the soft spine and makes the bait more flexible, so that it will have a more enticing swimming action and will be less likely to twist in the water.

Now you're ready to rig the ballyhoo to the hook.

Hold the ballyhoo in your left hand, and with your left thumb lift up the gill cover.

With your right hand, insert the hook point under the gills, into the body cavity. Work the point as far back as you can (bending the ballyhoo with your left hand helps here), and bring the point out on the underside of the bait.

When the point emerges, pull on it gently—just enough to bring the eye of the hook under the gill cover, and the leader pin under the "chin" of the ballyhoo, forward of the eyes.

Insert the pin upward, through both jaws of the bait, and with your thumb, hold the leader wire flush against the underside of the "chin."

Take the copper wire and wrap it tightly around the entire head TWICE behind the pin. Now wrap the copper wire around the head in front of the pin, and continue spiraling the wraps down the ballyhoo's bill for its full length. Keep all wraps snug, and finish by making your last couple of wraps very tight and close together near the end of the bill. Or, if you have a lot of excess copper wire, spiral some of it back up the bill toward the head again.

There is no exact routine for wrapping the copper wire, so don't worry about whether you have each wrap "just right." The important points are simply to have the head wrapped tightly so the pin will not slip out, and the bill wrapped snugly to the leader.

Your ballyhoo is now rigged and ready for trolling. It should skip the surface, or "swim" through the water without twisting. If it does twist, then an adjustment is necessary, so crank the bait in.

Usually, a twisting bait means there is pressure on the hook. It can be relieved by taking a knife point and enlarging the hole where the hook protrudes. Simply make a short slit with the knife point, thus extending the hole toward the head of the bait, in front of the hook.

NOTE ON HOOK SIZES: Ballyhoo come in various sizes, from about six inches long to more than a foot. Size of the average ballyhoo is around 10 inches. You may wish to buy both small and large ones for different purposes. Then, too, there are times you have to take what you can get, regardless of your preference. Because of this, you should keep at least three different hook sizes handy for your ballyhoo rigging.

The O'Shaughnessy is by far the best hook pattern for rigging ballyhoo, because the long shank allows the hook to be positioned farther aft in the bait.

For those tiny ballyhoo use a 5/0 or 6/0 hook; for average-size bait, a 7/0 or 8/0; for the largest ballyhoo, a 9/0 or 10/0.

ALTERNATE RIG: THE RUBBER BAND

In rigging the ballyhoo, you may leave out the copper wire and use a tiny rubber band to hold the pin tightly in place. Drop the rubber band on the pin, stretch it around the head, and drop the other end over the pin. It may be necessary to stretch the rubber band twice around the head to assure a tight grip.

When using the rubber band instead of the copper wire, break the ballyhoo's bill off at the base.

Aside from substituting the rubber band for copper wire, this rig is made exactly the same way as previously described.

ALTERNATE RIG: THE BEAD CHAIN

The bead-chain rig comes ready-made and is purchased, complete with instructions, in your tackle store. Therefore, the rig is not illustrated here.

With the bead-chain, your hook is positioned near the tail of the bait, rather than forward. You insert the bait-needle in the ballyhoo's vent, and run the needle out the mouth. With the needle, you pull the bead-chain through, leaving the hook in position at the extreme rear of the abdominal cavity. Copper wire then is used to anchor the chain at the head, so there will be no pressure on the hook.

DOUBLE-HOOK BALLYHOO

A double-hook ballyhoo rig really isn't very satisfactory for trolling because the added hook seriously hampers the bait's action. Moreover, the second hook isn't necessary for most offshore fish and, in fact, can be a disadvantage in billfishing.

You may however, use a double hook when drift-fishing—especially for king mackerel, which have an uncanny knack for severing the ballyhoo just in back of the single hook.

The rig shown here is the easiest of all double-hook rigs.

The second hook goes AFTER the bait is completely rigged—do not put it on before you rig, or you will be unable to rig in regular fashion at all.

Slip the eye of the second hook over the point of the first one then press the point of the second hook upward into the bait. The flesh of a ballyhoo is soft, and the teeth of a kingfish sharp. He will get hooked even though the point of the hook is buried.

There are two main ways of attaching the second hook:

1. Pry open the eye of the second hook, then press the eye closed again with pliers after the hook is in place.

2. With pliers, bend down the barb of the first hook just enough to permit the eye of the second to slip over it. Then pry the barb back to its original position with the blade of a screwdriver.

SWIMMING OR LEADED BALLYHOO

A dead ballyhoo can be made to "swim" just under the surface instead of skipping the top. This rig is valuable for days when the seas are so rough that skipping baits seem to stay airborne longer than they stay in the water. And even in good weather, the swimming ballyhoo gives your spread an additional enticement that may well get some strikes from fish that ignore the skippers.

Rigging the swimming ballyhoo is essentially the same as rigging the normal, skipping ballyhoo. The obvious difference is that a sinker must be incorporated into your rig at the time when you wrap the hook to the wire. The sinker weighs from one-half to perhaps one ounce, depending on the size of the ballyhoo and the sea conditions. Heavier sinkers will NOT provide any substantially deeper running depth.

First, slide an egg sinker onto your leader wire, running it up the wire and out of the way. Then run the wire through your hook eye and make about six haywire twists.

Now bring the sinker tight against the wraps and then continue making haywire twists ahead of the sinker. Make at least six more haywires, and finish off with several overhand wraps, leaving an upright "pin" of wire, just as in the basic ballyhoo rig.

Before hooking the ballyhoo, it's especially important to bend it several times to break the spine, for maximum suppleness. Use a bit of extra effort to position the hook as far back in the bait as possible. This will assure that the sinker comes to rest under the "chin" of the ballyhoo.

The pin can now be pushed through the head, bottom to top, and the rig completed exactly as with the unleaded ballyhoo.

FINGER MULLET, CIGAR MINNOW

This is the rig to use with finger mullet, cigar minnows or other small fish you may wish to troll.

Almost any type of small fish makes an acceptable trolling bait in an emergency, and if you get the chance to fish in foreign waters you might be faced with having to rig an unfamiliar species. Study the shape of the fish and the contour of its head, then decide whether to rig it in the fashion of the ballyhoo, or in the manner described here.

With this rig you do not use a "pin" of leader wire. In fact, you do not even attach your hook to the leader in advance.

Lay your hook alongside the bait, with the eye of the hook even with the eye of the fish. This is how you measure the approximate place where the hook point will come out of the fish's belly. Take the point of a knife and make a small slit in the belly at that spot.

Now insert the eye of the hook through that slit, into the belly, then forward through the throat and into the mouth.

Run the leader wire through the bottom jaw, through the eye of the hook, through the top jaw and out the top of the head. Pull enough wire through for ease of wrapping.

Last, wrap your leader wire close in front of the fish's lips, using the Haywire twist. Finish the wrap and break off excess.

As you can see, the pull will be on the loop of wire through the bait's head. There should be no pull on the hook. If the bait tends to twist, enlarge the hook hole with a knife point. It also helps to flex the bait back and forth to break the spine in one or more places.

LARGE MULLET

Large mullet are rigged in essentially the same way as finger mullet. However, the backbone must be removed, and there is some sewing involved.

You'll need a de-Boner (available in tackle stores) and a bait needle. Floss or any kind of small braided line may be used as "sewing thread."

Large mullet are mainly employed in marlin and tuna fishing, but they take smaller species as well (to the distress of folks after big game). A large rigged mullet also makes a great bait for deep trolling in quest of amberjack and heavy grouper.

TO PREPARE THE BAIT: Remove the entire backbone with the de-boner. If you haven't used one before, don't fret. It is much like coring an apple. The de-boner is a hollow tube with a sharp edge. Insert the edge under the gill, get it into position in front of the backbone, pointing toward the tail. With a slow, twisting motion, work the de-boner back for almost the full length of the fish. Bend the tail of the fish sideways and make a last gentle push with the de-boner to sever the spine. Remove the de-boner and the entire backbone comes with it. A rod (supplied with the de-boner when you buy it) is used to expel the backbone.

Now make a slit in the belly, large enough so that you can remove all the mullet's entrails. Insert the eye of your hook in this slit and push it forward into position inside the mullet's mouth, directly under the eyes. Insert your leader wire through both jaws and through the eye of the hook, exactly as with the finger mullet. Make your leader wrap as before.

It is now necessary to tie the gills closed, so that trolling pressure will not tear the bait. You CAN simply tie a piece of string tightly around the head, in back of the eyes, to hold the gills down. To avoid all chance of slippage, however, run your string through the mullet's head, using your bait needle, and then tie the string off tightly under the head.

If the belly slit you made in removing the entrails is so large that it seems likely to catch water and tear while trolling, then use your needle to sew the belly slit closed.

LEADED OR SWIMMING MULLET

To make the mullet remain under the surface and "swim," you incorporate an egg sinker into the rigging, much as for the ballyhoo rig already described.

The leaded mullet was the standard bait for giant bluefin tuna in the heyday of that Bahamas fishery. Many marlin anglers and pot-luck offshore trollers like to troll both leaded and unleaded mullet baits at the same time. In rough seas, where skipping baits might be in the air as much as in the water, the lead helps keep the baits where they belong.

Obviously, finger mullet and cigar minnows can also be leaded if the angler desires, but with a smaller sinker, of course.

TO RIG THE LEAD: Slide your egg sinker onto the leader wire before inserting the wire through the head of the fish and the hook. After the wire is inserted through the bait and in position for wrapping, slide the sinker down and hold it under the bait's "chin" while you make as tight a wrap as possible.

Size of the egg sinker varies, but is usually one or two ounces with large mullet; one-half to one ounce with finger mullet.

RIGGING MACKEREL, BARRACUDA

Mackerel, small barracuda, small bonefish and other species can be rigged with hook inside, exactly the same way as for mullet. All make good trolling baits for larger species of game fish, especially

163

marlin. Bonefish are not used in Florida, of course, because of both protective laws and angler attitudes, but small ones are plentiful in many tropical locales around the world.

With mackerel and small barracuda it usually is not necessary to de-bone, as you can make the bait limber enough simply by flexing it and breaking the spine in several places. De-boning is not so necessary for baits intended to skip the surface, as it is for baits intended to "swim."

Whether to de-bone or not, in a given situation and with a given bait, is largely your own decision.

In almost every case, however, it will be necessary to sew or tie the gills closed. With mackerel, you should also sew the belly cavity around the hook, even if your original hook-slit is not large. Mackerel flesh is very soft and tears easily.

MARLIN RIG, HOOK OUTSIDE

In marlin fishing, the larger baits such as mackerel, bonito, bonefish, jack, dolphin, etc. are frequently rigged with the hook outside the bait. This rig is especially desirable when seeking the biggest possible marlin on 80 and 130-lb.-test line, and when using the biggest of gamefish hooks—12/0 to 15/0, or even 20/0. It is sometimes used with smaller baits, smaller hooks and light or medium tackle, but a rig with the hook inside is generally chosen for those applications.

With giant bait and an outside hook, the baitfish normally requires no preparation at all. You use it as is, with no de-boning or cutting—although the gills and mouth should be sewed tight.

TO RIG THE OUTSIDE HOOK: Take your bait needle, and thread a length of braided line through the eye sockets of the fish, remove the needle and tie the line tightly. Leave the ends of the sewing line long enough so they can be wrapped two or three times around the bend of your hook and tied again.

Some anglers rig in this same way, although running the tying line through both lips of the fish, instead of through the eye sockets. Most, however, prefer the eye tieup.

A BETTER METHOD THAN EITHER is to use a metal figure-eight as an attachment between the hook and the eye tieup. This method is explained under the instructions for rigging live bonito.

Refer to that section, as the rig is exactly the same whether the bait is alive or dead.

EEL FOR TROLLING

To rig an eel for trolling, first wrap your hook to the leader wire, using the Haywire twist. Then place the bend of the hook at the eel's vent and measure the wire so you can wrap on a swivel at the mouth. Once the swivel is affixed to the other end of the short wire, insert a bait needle into the vent and use it to pull the swivel through the body cavity and into position in the mouth.

Sew the back eye of the swivel securely to the mouth, wrapping the thread tightly around the head as well. Make sure there is no pull at the hook: enlarge the opening slightly with a knife point if necessary. With a Haywire twist, attach your leader to the front eye of the swivel.

In addition to being a great bait for offshore big-game fish, the rigged eel is excellent closer to shore for striped bass, blues and even big snook.

RIGGING AN EELSKIN

Here's the "plumber's special"—the main components being a length of brass chain and a rubber stopper with lip. The hooks can be affixed with split rings or double-ended snaps. The preserved eel

—skin is simply fitted over the chain and tied snugly behind the lip of the stopper, with hooks positioned one near the front and the other at the rear. A couple of small slits in the tough eelskin at the head permit water to enter and fill out the shriveled skin as you troll—making it quite fresh and lifelike in appearance.

SQUID FOR DRIFTING ONLY

As you can see, this is basically an application of the all-purpose Stinger Rig shown in Chapter 3. Two single hooks are rigged as shown, either with wire or monofilament. The hook size must be gauged according to the size of the squid, and so must the distance between the hooks.

Insert the point of the front hook into the end of the tail, and out as shown. The rear hook is simply pushed through the head of the bait from the underside.

When drifting at night for swordfish, this rig is entirely adequate, and holds up well because there is no heavy pressure on the bait. Still, most professional skippers who swordfish by drifting at night do rig their baits as carefully as for trolling. Maybe its mostly for the sake of their image.

SQUID FOR TROLLING OR DRIFTING

Small rigged squids are one of the most popular baits for white marlin, and squids are effective as well for most species of billfish and tuna. Larger squids, of course, are used with bigger hooks for giants such as blue marlin and swordfish. Large squids, rigged in this fashion, are pretty much standard in the once-and-hopefully-future sport of night-drifting for swordfish, which originated in Florida but has now spread to many other coastal areas of the U.S. and abroad. Note, though, that drifting does not put nearly so much pressure on a bait as does trolling. The preceding rig is much faster to make and can be used instead of this one for drifting.

To rig the trolling squid, you must first measure with hook and leader so that you can tie or wrap in a small egg sinker at the point where it will snug up against the squid's "tail," with the hook in position in the head just in front of its juncture with the mantle.

Insert a bait needle into the firm part of the head, between the eyes, and draw the leader inside the mantle its full length until the sinker comes into illustrated position. Sew the mantle to the leader, and reinforce the connection of head to mantle at the places marked, with X-shaped stitches.

THE TROLLING STRIP

A properly-rigged strip is one of the best trolling baits. Private anglers seldom make use of it because it is more bother to rig than a ballyhoo, but many of the more successful charter captains insist on keeping a strip out at all times (in combination with other baits), and the strip frequently outfishes the rest.

As with ballyhoo, the strip rig requires a "pin" of leader wire. But note that in this case the pin points in the same direction as the hook, and you leave a much longer pin than for ballyhoo.

The most desirable strips are those cut from the white under-parts of a bonito. Belly sections of mackerel, kings, dolphin, barracuda and other fish can be used. Mullet strips work well but are less durable.

The strip should be about 10 or 12 inches long and trimmed to teardrop shape—with a short taper at the hook end; a longer taper at the rear. Carefully trim off excess flesh so that the strip is no more than a quarter-inch thick, preferably less than that. The thinner the strip, the more action. But a thin layer of flesh must be maintained so the bait will hold shape.

TO RIG THE STRIP: Insert the pin through the strip at the short-tapered front end. Study the illustrations and note that the pin must now be bent forward and secured on the leader, ahead of the bait. To do this, take pliers and bend a tiny V-shaped or U-shaped catch at the end of the pin, so that it can be fixed to the leader in much the same manner as a safety pin.

Now the strip must be bunched forward slightly while you insert the hook. After the hook is in place, the strip must lie perfectly flat. There must be no pressure from the hook on the strip. If there is, enlarge the hook hole with a knife point to relieve the pressure.

Cut Baits

GULF COAST BOTTOM RIG

This used to be the standard bait for tarpon fishing over much of the Gulf Coast. It also has taken many very big snook, and also is probably the best dead bait for sharks. It is fished directly on bottom, lying there until picked up. When a fish takes this bait, allow him to travel with it as you keep your reel in freespool. After a few seconds, tighten your line gently, then strike hard.

This rig should no longer be used for tarpon, unless your plan is

168

to kill and keep the fish, for most tarpon caught this way are hooked deep. Check the laws! Keeping a tarpon in Florida requires an expensive permit.

For this rig, make up your leader in advance. Use a six-foot leader of 100 or 120-pound-test monofilament, or a six-foot leader of 90 or 135-pound-test wire cable.

If monofilament is used, tie a stout swivel to one end of the leader, a 10/0 hook to the other. The ties can be made with either the Improved Clinch Knot or the Two-Wrap Hangman's Knot. In either case, use pliers and a lot of pressure to make sure the knots are drawn down tight.

If cable is used, attach the hook and swivel with sleeve and crimper.

TO RIG: Cut the head off a mullet. Run a bait needle the full length of the mullet, alongside the backbone coming out at the tail. Hook the eye of the needle to your swivel and pull your complete leader through the bait, so the hook is positioned as shown.

CUT FISH

Cut baits and unrigged whole dead baits are used for still-fishing, and occasionally for drifting. They differ, as a class, from rigged baits in that they are not calculated to give an appearance of live action. Nor is any special rigging necessary. You simply stick the bait on your hook and start fishing.

Mullet is commonly used fish for cut bait, because it is widely available and inexpensive. The same for menhaden. You can also cut baits from most any kind of fish you might catch with the cut mullet. Naturally, the fish you don't want to take home are the ones you're most inclined to cut up for bait—pinfish or sailor's choice, ladyfish, jack, small grunts, etc.

However, if you get in a tight spot for bait, don't hesitate to cut baits from one of your "eating" fish. For instance, if you're drifting for speckled trout and run out of bait, you can cut some strips from the belly of trout in your ice box and go right on catching fish.

HOW TO CUT BAIT: Always use a cutting board and a sharp knife. The fish may or may not be scaled, but scaling usually helps. Slice fillets from both sides of the fish, discard the rest (unless you wish to use the head for bait).

From each fillet you can cut squarish slabs of bait for bottom fishing, or rather narrow strips for drift fishing.

STRIP FOR DRIFTING

If drift-fishing (speckled trout, etc.) take a rough-cut strip and hook it through one end, as shown in the illustration. There is no need to rig the strip, or taper it, as you would for trolling.

STRIP OR CHUNK FOR BOTTOM FISHING

If bottom-fishing, use either a rough strip or a chunk and run your hook through the bait twice (three or more times if using a bait large enough to permit it).

"SHINER TAIL" STRIPS

Good baits for either trolling or bottom fishing can be cut from small fish such as pinfish. These are called "shiner tails" and widely used in seatrout-fishing. But these baits produce a variety of fish in many waters.

One illustration shows a single bait, cut diagonally from the tail. The other shows how you can cut the entire tail half from the pinfish, then cut it again lengthwise to make two baits. With either method, you cut all the way through the fish (that is, you don't just slice off one fillet), and use the bait with bone in.

Such a bait is more durable than a strip of fillet, since it withstands the nibbles of "bait stealers" while waiting for a good strike.

HOOK POSITION: If bottom fishing, place the hook near the center of the bait as shown in the illustrations. If drifting, position the hook close to the "head" end of the bait.

MULLET HEAD

The head of a mullet, hooked both lips as shown and fished patiently on bottom, is an excellent bait for snapper and grouper on the reefs, or for snook, tarpon, jewfish, etc., inshore. Snook do not hit a dead bait as readily as a live one, but some big snook are often caught on mullet heads. Obviously, you can use other kinds of fish heads too.

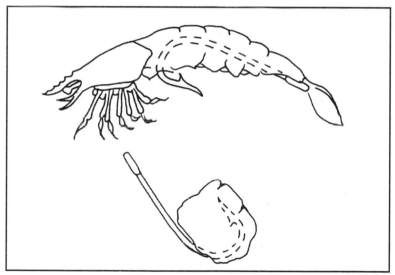

DEAD SHRIMP

Dead shrimp may be used whole, broken in half, or cut in small pieces.

If used whole, thread the shrimp on the hook as shown. Half a shrimp should be threaded in much the same way.

For panfish or baitfish, use tiny pieces of shrimp, with the skin peeled off, and cover the point of the hook as illustrated.

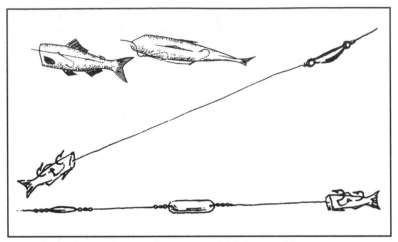

CUT PLUG BAIT FOR MOOCHING

To rig a herring or similar baitfish for "mooching" in the traditional style of salmon fishermen in the Northwest, first cut off the head, slanting the cut slightly rearward. Remove entrails. Now use our old friend, the Stinger Rig, shown in Chapter 3. Again, hook size must be appropriate to the size of the bait. Insert the front hook in at the head and out the side. The rear hook goes in and out either the side of the fish or the dorsal surface.

The mooching bait is drifted out and is worked by the current in an erratic, wobbling and spinning motion. Or it may be slow trolled. In either case it can be rigged to a weightless leader when conditions permit, but more often is used in combination with a trolling sinker to obtain the desired depth, as in the second illustration. The third drawing shows how a flasher or dodger can be incorporated into the leader ahead of the plug bait for additional attraction.

Bait-Lure Combinations

FEATHER AND STRIP

An extremely popular combination for trolling offshore or on the reef is the feather-strip.

The trolling feather is threaded to your leader, after which you rig a strip for trolling as described earlier. In use, the feather slides down to the hook, covering the forward portion of the strip.

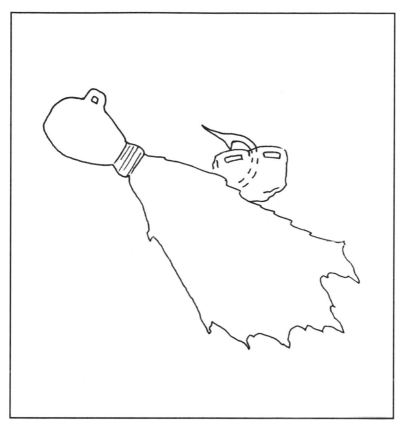

JIG WITH SHRIMP

When you add a small "tip" of cut shrimp to an artificial jig you come up with the one best casting lure on the Gulf Coast. The same combo clicks for bonefish, and much Atlantic Coast fishing as well.

You will catch many more redfish and trout with a tipped jig than with a bare jig. You will also catch bottom-feeders, such as sheepshead and drum, which rarely if ever hit a plain jig. At the same time, the tip of shrimp does not hinder the action of the bait and so you catch just as many snook and tarpon—maybe more, although this is a point of debate among anglers.

But to make the jig work right, you have to use a small piece of shrimp. Too large a piece causes the jig to twist on the retrieve.

You get more tips from a single shrimp if you cut them with a knife, rather than breaking them off with your fingers.

JIG WITH STRIP

A small strip of cut fish or squid can be used in place of the shrimp. It does not work so well as the shrimp for a wide range of Gulf Coast fish, but often pays off handsomely when you're fishing for mackerel or bluefish.

LARGE JIG WITH BALLYHOO
OR CIGAR MINNOW

A heavy jig, weighing two to four ounces, can be fitted with a second hook and rigged with a ballyhoo or cigar minnow as shown to make a most productive bait for deep drift fishing.

To attach the second hook, you can use either of two methods:

1. Pry open the eye of the second hook, slip the eye over the barb of the first hook, and press the eye closed.

2. With pliers, bend down the barb of the hook slightly—just enough to permit the eye of the second hook to slide over it. Then pry the barb back into position, using the blade of a screwdriver.

A lot of fishermen toss over this rig and let it go down deep—near bottom if depth permits, or at least 100 feet if fishing in deep blue water. They use the rig on a stout boat rod, and place the rod in a holder with the reel in gear, but the drag set fairly light. Most any fish which takes will hook itself. This rig has taken a great many big grouper, snapper, kingfish and even quite a few sailfish.

If kingfish are hitting, you may wish to add a third hook, since kings are notorious short-strikers. Rig the third hook exactly as you did the second.

LARGE JIG WITH STRIP

A deep jig with a strip can be used in precisely the same way as described for the ballyhoo—on a drifting line down deep.

But it is more frequently used as a king mackerel rig when kings are schooling, and is one of the best. Use a nylon jig, weighing one or one-and-a-half ounces. Attach a second hook (see above for methods), and hook on the strip as shown.

Cast it out, let it sink to or beyond the suspected level of the kingfish, then retrieve it with sweeps of the rod. Kings will hit it while it sinks, or during the retrieve.

There is also a good rig for bottom jigging. Let it sink all the way to bottom, then bounce it around a few times without retrieving any line. If a grouper or snapper is around, chances are he'll hit. If no strike occurs at bottom, retrieve all the way to the boat with sharp upward sweeps of the rod, cranking in line between sweeps. You can catch kings or other mid-depth species on the way in.

176

Chapter 9

Baits Rigs & Tackle

Artificial Lures

TROLLING FEATHERS AND SKIRTED LURES

For want of a more widely-used term, trolling lures which feature a weighted head in combination with some kind of soft trailer material are frequently called "feathers."

The principal difference between "feathers" and lead-head jigs is that the feathers are supplied without a built-in hook, whereas jigs have the hook molded into the head.

Often the trailer material is really of feathers, and at one time all such lures were made with feathers—hence the popular name, which has hung on. Nowadays, nylon is commonly used as trailer material (example: the Sea Witch.) This type lure is also made with plastic streamers and, rarely, with hair.

Feathers come in a wide assortment of sizes, and are used mostly for offshore trolling. You run your leader wire through the hollow head, and attach the hook of your choice.

The feather is often rigged in combination with a strip of bait, as described previously.

Any ocean gamefish will at times hit the plain trolled feather, and for a lot of offshore species, the feather alone seems just about as productive as the feather-strip combination.

Most popular colors are solid yellow, solid white, or mixtures of either color with red.

DODGERS, FLASHERS, BELLS

A variety of shiny ornaments strung ahead of the trolled lure have proven effective for many different kinds of gamefish, and in far-flung areas. Though most-used in deep trolling for trout and salmon—on the Pacific Coast, in the Great Lakes and other deep lakes—these elaborate setups also have proved their mettle in salt-water for bluefish and other species.

As illustrated, the large metal flashers and dodgers are built into the leader by means of swivels at each end of the device. The strings of spinners or wobblers generally are purchased ready-made, although a few anglers do rig up their own.

The illustrations show a spoon and a streamer fly as the trailing lures, but many other lures can be used too. Let preferences of the various fishing areas guide you on this.

To get the rig deep, a bank or dipsey swivel is used on a dropper line, as shown.

TROLLING SPOONS

Perhaps the most versatile of all saltwater trolling lures is the silver spoon. Many models, in many sizes, are made by a number of different manufacturers. Most popular trolling spoons have fixed single hooks.

Size designation for saltwater trolling spoons are by number. Most-used sizes are between No. 1 (small) and No. 7 (large). Bigger spoons than No. 7 may be used for giant tarpon, or for off-shore species.

Unfortunately, those numbers denote relative size only in spoons of the same brand. One company's No. 2 may be another company's No. 5.

Another way to gauge spoon size is by hook size. Most spoons do name the hook size on their packaging.

Here is a short table which may help you select a spoon of appropriate size:

Type Fishing	Hook Size
Inshore trolling (mackerel, blues, etc.)	1/0 - 3/0
Inshore trolling (snook, reds, small tarpon)	3/0 - 6/0
Offshore trolling (kingfish, etc.)	6/0 and up
Big tarpon trolling	6/0 - 9/0

This table is a general guideline. Variations are common among different anglers.

Some spoons come with a built-on swivel. You should always use a swivel ahead of a spoon to help reduce line twist, so if your spoon has no swivel, be sure to use one between leader and line. If twist persists when using a barrel swivel—as well it might—switch to a ballbearing swivel, the most positive kind.

See the Wire-Wrapping section for a special rig that provides extra action when trolling a spoon.

See more about spoons in upcoming section on casting lures.

TEASERS AND BIRDS

Teasers are oversized lures without hooks, used to make a commotion while trolling and thus entice marlin, sails and other sought-after gamefish to the vicinity of your trolled baits.

Almost every experienced skipper likes to use a teaser while billfishing.

Manufactured teasers may simply be huge wooden plugs, or wooden plugs with trailing skirts of nylon. Empty bottles or empty cans with holes punched in both ends are often used as teasers.

The teaser is rigged to a heavy wire leader, which in turn is tied, by means of a big swivel, to a stout rope or cord. The cord is snubbed around a cleat on the transom of the boat. Most teasers are trolled only 20 feet or so behind the boat.

BIRDS originally were large teasers designed with airplane-like wings that gave them a splashing, in-and-out-of-the-water action similar to flying fish. Birds now are available in many different models and sizes. They are frequently used as lures, or as a small teaser built right into the trolling rig (usually at the point where leader joins line). Like artificial squids, small birds can also be rigged in a daisy chain, then pulled as a multiple teaser.

OCEAN TROLLING PLUGS

Any diving or sinking plug can be trolled as well as cast. Almost all plugs trolled inshore are simply casting plugs (crankbaits or floater-divers) of popular models.

A few very large plugs are manufactured specifically for saltwater trolling—mainly for tarpon but also for offshore species.

Though not used nearly as often as they should be by veteran offshore anglers, big plugs with extra-strength hooks produce a lot of strikes from wahoo and king mackerel. And plugs which run deep are surprisingly effective over the reefs for grouper and snapper.

OFFSHORE TROLLING LURES

Big-game fishermen in all waters of the world are turning more and more to artificial lures for deep-sea trolling. Long used in Hawaii and other waters of the Pacific, lures are now well established, too, on most marlin grounds of the South Atlantic, Gulf of Mexico and Caribbean.

Typically, the big marlin lures feature a hard plastic head and a plastic skirt. There are several basic head designs, each providing a different action and each generally requiring a different range of trolling speeds to bring out its best performance. Tapered or torpedo heads offer the least water resistance. They are straight runners and can be trolled at the fastest speeds. Flathead lures are currently the most popular style in most big-game areas. They also run straight, but their blunt heads kick up more commotion. Flatheads can be used at high speeds—up to 20 knots—although most anglers prefer to drag them at about 9 or 10 knots. Lures with a slanted, concave head, such as the long-familiar Konaheads, have an erratic, darting action, and for this reason are often used as teasers as well as actual lures. Because they aren't straight runners, they are usually pulled at the low end of the lure-speed range, eight knots or so, although somewhat faster speeds may be used.

Artificial lures in general eliminate the "drop-back," which is standard procedure in attempting to hook a billfish which strikes a natural rigged bait. Marlin will often track an artificial, but just as often, the strike comes suddenly and savagely, and the fish is either on or off before the angler has much chance to influence the result. Note, though, that fish are not so quick to drop the softer trolling lures and a modest amount of drop-back with those can be helpful.

Trolling lures may be trolled directly off the rod, with the reel in strike-drag position. But most veteran anglers and captains much prefer to provide an elastic resistance to a striking fish. This they do by running a "stinger" line off the outrigger line. At the end of the stinger line is a heavy-duty snap. A rubber band is half-hitched

Sevenstrand Clone

Boone Striker

Konahead

Moldcraft Soft Heads

to the fishing line and then the other end of the band is placed in the snap on the stinger line. When a marlin hits, both the "give" of the outrigger lines and the rubber band provide shock-absorption and yet there is enough pressure to set the hook before the line cuts through the rubber band and breaks it.

After the fishing line comes tight to the fish, additional hooksetting tactics of a traditional nature can be employed—gunning the engines briefly and striking with the rod.

RIGGING THE TROLLING LURES

Many of the different brands of offshore or marlin lures are available either rigged or unrigged. For real aficionados, of course, rigging is part of the game and they prefer to do it themselves.

Single-strand wire is so seldom used that it can be shunted aside. There are several reasons for this, but the possibility of kink-breakage, particularly with erratic lures, is probably the main one. With big artificial lures either very heavy monofilament or wire cable is the choice. Monofilament wins out in popularity because of the general feeling that mono leaders, in any kind of fishing, draw more strikes than do wire leaders. Also, mono is more easily handled at boatside during the gaffing, tagging or release process.

There are nearly as many variations in rigging preferences as there are in lures. If you haven't developed your own preferences, try the following procedure:

Hooks should be of forged, big-game patterns. In the rig to be described, ring-eye hooks (with ring braised, of course) are best. Sizes range from 10/0 to about 14/0. The gap of the hook—or of the leading hook in the two-hook setup to be described—should be about as wide as the head of the lure, or a bit wider. The trailing hook can be exactly the same, although many anglers prefer it to be one or two sizes smaller.

In addition to the hooks, you will need 300-pound monofilament for leader, 600-pound aircraft cable for joining the two hooks, a crimping tool and No. 11 sleeves.

Cut a piece of the monofilament to your chosen leader length. IGFA rules allow 30 feet in line classes heavier than 20 (with a 10-foot double line). To avoid later measurement problems caused by stretch and/or careless measuring to begin with, make the leader about 25 feet long.

"Ball" one end of the mono leader by holding a flame to it and pressing the heated end against a metallic object. Then form a simple loop at this same end and crimp it as described in the section on leaders. Some anglers use a single sleeve, others two. If carefully crimped, a single should suffice. The other end of the leader is left alone for the present. It will later be threaded through the lure and crimped to the pre-rigged double hooks. And now to rigging the hooks:

Cut a piece of aircraft cable six or eight inches long. Run one end through the eye of the forward hook and crimp it. The other end is crimped to the eye of the trailing hook. A single loop and single sleeve is used in both these crimps, as in the first drawing on page

81. To conform to IGFA rules, the eyes of the two hooks must be at least a hook's length apart and the trailing hook cannot extend more than a hook's length beyond the skirt of the lure.

Last, use electrician's tape to tape the cable tightly to the shank of the leading hook. Again, preferences as to the relative planes of the two hook-points vary, but most often the taping is done in such a way as to position the point of the trailing hook at right angles to the front one.

With several leaders prepared in advance, along with several of these two-hook sets, you can choose or change lures easily—having only to run the mono leader through the lure and crimp on the hooks.

SQUIDS AND OTHER MOLDED BAITS

Imitations of popular natural baits, molded of soft plastic, can be found nowadays on many tackle counters. They include ballyhoo, mullet, flying fish, squid, dolphin and even plain strips. Some are ready-rigged with short leaders.

By far the most commercially successful of these molded baits have been the squids, obtainable from several different manufacturers and in a variety of sizes and colors. Trolled plastic squids will take all the popular offshore gamefish. Though not widely used in this manner, artificial squid can also be drifted with effect, and even used for inshore casting. Quite a few sailfish, and even a number of swordfish, have been caught on drifted plastic squids.

DAISY CHAIN: Squids are often rigged into "daisy chains"—a string of three, four or more on a single leader—and used either as a teaser or, in some cases, as an actual trolling lure.

Rigging a daisy chain is easy. Just thread the desired number of squids onto a wire or heavy monofilament leader, then space them the desired distance apart—generally a foot or two—by fixing small RubberCor sinkers at the selected spacing locations. A hook at the end of the leader completes the rig. No hook is added, of course, if the chain is to serve simply as a teaser.

Artificial Casting Lures

The term "artificial lure" or simply "artificial," refers to any device made of synthetic material that is intended to fool a fish into thinking it is natural food.

All artificials require some sort of motion to make them work. Usually the motion is provided either by casting the lure and retrieving it, or by trolling. Some lures work well with no more motion than merely allowing them to sink or settle slowly in the water. Others must be moved fast to draw strikes.

This section will cover artificial lures used mostly for casting, but often for trolling. Many models of artificial lures can be—and are—used in salt and fresh water. With most of the others, the only difference between fresh and saltwater versions is in size, and perhaps in hook strength.

Certain artificial lures designed strictly for saltwater trolling have been covered already.

Obviously, there are far too many different lures to permit a comprehensive survey. Instead, this section will look at the major types of lures and discuss some of their uses. The lures mentioned and/or illustrated are given only as examples of types. They are well-known models, but not necessarily recommended over similar ones of other makes.

186

SURFACE AND FLOATING-DIVING PLUGS

Surface lures are the pets of many bass, pike and muskie fishermen, as well as a lot of saltwater anglers. They are designed to splash the top of the water and imitate a distressed fish. Some surface plugs make more noise than others, according to design. And some surface plugs float while at rest, but dive under and "swim" on a straight retrieve. These are called floating-diving plugs and can be used either as a surface lure or underwater lure.

THE SLIM-MINNOW TYPES: These are slender, buoyant plugs with small plastic lips. Some, such as the original Rapalas, are made of balsa wood, and some—for instance the slender Rebels—are made of plastic.

The balsa wood models have a bit more action, and are preferred by many freshwater fishermen. Plastic ones are tougher and better suited for use in the sea. However, the plastic ones do work very well in fresh water, and many inland anglers prefer them if for no other reason than that they are much easier to cast.

Several good retrieves are possible with this type plug. Try twitching them on the surface two or three times with pauses in between. Also try retrieving them VERY slowly, so that they "swim" but stay atop the water. You can also impart a fast, darting retrieve to them by sweeping your rod as you wind in. Or you can simply crank at medium to fast speed and treat them as swimming, underwater lures.

As surface lures, the slender minnows really shine when the water is very calm. A noisier surface plug might scare more fish than it attracts.

THE DARTING TYPES: These are wooden or plastic plugs, designed so they will dig slightly into the water and dart when the rod is jerked. They are often referred to as jerk baits because one common retrieve is to jerk them sharply, with only an instant's pause between jerks. They dive by virtue of small lips, which may either be designed into the head itself, or added. Examples include the Creek Chub Darter, Boone Spinana, Lucky 13 and Bass Oreno. Darters have for many years been a standby lure of both bass and snook casters. They also work well on tarpon and many other fresh and saltwater fish.

In fresh water, these plugs normally are allowed to lie still for up to a minute, then twitched two or three times with pauses in between. On the retrieve, plugs of this type dive under the surface and swim seductively, becoming shallow crankbaits.

Many strikes come during this stage.

The standard saltwater action is much the same, except that little, if any, pause is allowed between jerks of the rod. This is an especially good lure for mangrove snook. The initial noise of the darter seems to draw them from under the roots. They might hit while the plug is being worked at the surface but, just as often, they strike during the final retrieve—possibly because they think the distressed fish has recovered and is escaping.

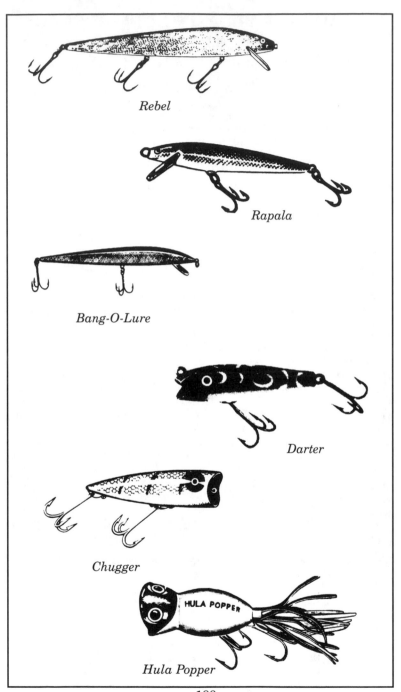

Rebel

Rapala

Bang-O-Lure

Darter

Chugger

HULA POPPER

Hula Popper

THE POPPING TYPES: True popping plugs have hollowed or cup-faced heads (Example: Chugger, Plunker, Hula Popper). They make a loud "blurping" noise when jerked hard with the rod, but the angler can control the amount of noise by how softly or sharply he twitches his rod to cause the pop.

In fresh water, a rather soft pop is preferred, with a long pause before the next one. Sometimes, however, a loud pop pays off better —especially if there is considerable chop on the water.

The pop-and-pause retrieve is good, too, for shallow-water fishing along the coast.

Large popping plugs are one of the very best, and most exciting, of lures for casting in deeper salt waters—such as the reefs, or even the Gulf Stream at times. Special large poppers—the Scudder is a good example—are used here, with heavy hooks that are wired through for strength.

For offshore fishing, you have to use a stout rod, and then pop the lure as hard as you can and as fast as you can. The more fuss the better. A big popper on the reefs can take just about anything, including barracuda, jack, amberjack, tuna, mackerel, kingfish, bonito, sailfish—and even big bottom fish such as grouper and snapper.

SURF POPPERS: These are slightly different popping lures, used mostly for long-distance casting from the surf in quest of striped bass and bluefish. Most of them actually are sinkers, or are neutrally buoyant, but a steady retrieve with a long surf rod keeps them blurping across the surface with a seductive and noisy action.

CRIPPLED MINNOW TYPES: These are somewhat similar to the darters, except they have no lips and most cannot dive at all. They are fitted with spinners, either at the tail or at both head and tail. (Examples: Torpedo, Dalton Special, Injured Minnow, Devil's Horse, Nip-i-Diddee.)

Though spinner-rigged plugs work in salt water, they have never become very popular. Most bass fishermen, however, keep some injured minnow plugs in their kits and use them avidly.

As with most freshwater surface plugs, this type works best with slow twitches and long pauses. Sometimes, especially at night, strikes come faster on a straight, slow retrieve with the propellers whirring steadily at the surface.

DANCING OR WALKING TYPES: These are torpedo shaped plugs, weighted slightly at the tail so they sit on the surface at an angle. The Zara Spook is a widely known and venerable example. Saltwater anglers often use a retrieve called "walking the dog" in which the plug is made to zig-sag across the surface by a fast retrieve combined with constant whipping of the rodtip. This tactic simulates a fleeing baitfish and is deadly for most saltwater predators, including stripers, bluefish, snook, jack and outsize seatrout.

Other good retrieves are possible, too. With steady cranking and a slower, rhythmic waving of the rodtip, they swim on the surface in more leisurely fashion, much like an undisturbed mullet.

Although "walking the dog" can produce violent strikes from bass

189

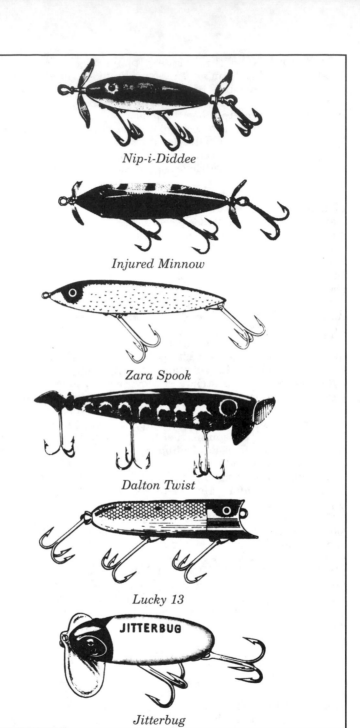

Nip-i-Diddee

Injured Minnow

Zara Spook

Dalton Twist

Lucky 13

Jitterbug

that are avidly feeding, bass anglers prefer a pop-and-pause retrieve with their Zaras and similar plugs, much the same as they use with other types of topwater baits. When the pop-and-pause technique is used with a dancing plug, it dives, then jumps high out of the water while remaining in almost the same spot.

FLOATING-DIVING PLUGS: The slim minnow already has been mentioned as a floater-diver. But there is another type which has been popular in fresh water for many years. The two leading examples are the Lucky 13 and Bass Oreno. They can be made to pop almost as loudly as a true popping plug, but dive well under the surface and wiggle enticingly on a fast retrieve.

CRAWLING PLUGS: Chief example of this type are the Crazy Crawler and the Jitterbug. Although they will draw strikes when fished in stop-and-go fashion, crawlers are most often worked with a straight, slow retrieve. They wobble or crawl across the surface with continuous noise and are much chosen for night fishing because bass, it seems, can zero in on them much better than on a lure which alternates noise and silence.

Bagley
Balsa B

Mann
Razor
Back

Bagley
Small Fry
Bass

Boone
Crankster

SHALLOW AND MEDIUM CRANKBAITS

Sub-surface plugs which require little action on the part of the angler other than winding the reel are called crankbaits. Most run at shallow or medium depth and they come in such a variety of shapes and configurations that they do not lend themselves to sub-classification so easily as did the surface lures. Therefore, such labels will not be used except in obvious instances.

Let's start with the plugs which sink by virtue of weight alone: that is, they have no lip or other planing device to help get them down.

Some of these plugs are slow-sinkers, the most famous of all per-

191

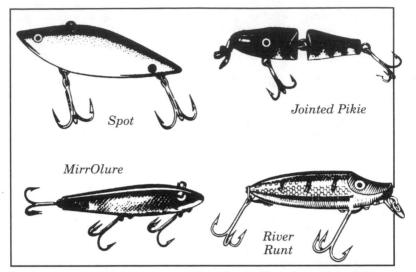

Spot

Jointed Pikie

MirrOlure

River Runt

haps—in salt water anyway—being the 52 M series of MirrOlures. This is one of the most versatile saltwater plugs of all for shallow fishing, and takes anything from trout to tarpon. MirrOlures of other series numbers are similar, but may vary in length, and in sinking rate.

Although MirrOlures are often fished in stop-and-go fashion, like a jerk bait, they do qualify as crankbaits because even the plain-head models swim enticingly on a steady, moderately fast retrieve. Some models have metal diving lips.

In fresh water, one widely popular family of underwater plugs is the "shad-type." These have the general appearance of small shad minnows—flattened and thin, but relatively deep-bodied. Some of the many examples include the Thin Fin and Spot. Some have molded-in lips that provide their swimming action. Others get their action from a slanted or vertically flattened head or a molded top fin. Anyway, all are shallow-running lures that take bass and a great variety of freshwater fish, and are excellent open-water lures. Most of them have counterpart models in their lines that are similar in size and action but run deeper.

Another prominent group, in much the same action category but vastly different appearance, are the "fat plugs" or "alphabet plugs"—so-called because they are, indeed, fat, and because the original models were named by single letters—such as "Big O" and "Big B." These are lipped plugs which generally float at rest, but which are not commonly employed as surface poppers, although they can produce fish as such. As a class they are shallow runners but, again, some models have larger lips for deeper diving.

This type plug is effective on a straight retrieve, although you should vary the speed to test for best results. There is nothing in particular to be gained by "jigging" your rod as you retrieve these lures; however, it often pays to impart a variable retrieve simply by cranking-and-stopping, cranking-and-stopping.

Let's move now to another group of shallow-to-medium plugs—those with rather short metal lips. Some famous examples are the River Runt, Pikie, L&S Lures and Cisco Kids. Their action is about the same as the shad types and others with molded lips. Some of them, particularly the Pikies, are old favorites in salt water as well as fresh, but usually in beefed-up models. They run a bit deeper on the average, than do the molded-lip plugs. Again, the best retrieve is a steady one with varying speeds.

Shallow-running plugs are excellent for trolling, as well as casting, whenever it isn't necessary to go down very deep. This holds for both salt and fresh water.

By trying different motor speeds to determine what pace brings out the best action, the unlipped MirrOlures are also great trolling baits for salt water.

Incidentally, many slow-sinking plugs can be fished effectively at great depth if you just take the time to let them sink before you retrieve. Try the "countdown" method: Count slowly as your plug sinks, and note the count on which it hits bottom. Next cast, shorten the count by one or two numbers, and you should be skimming close to the bottom. Keep the lure deep by pausing in the retrieve to allow it to sink once more.

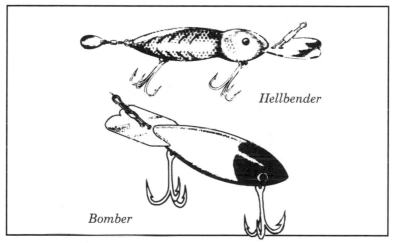

Hellbender

Bomber

DEEP-RUNNING CRANKBAITS

There are only two basic designs which can send a plug really deep—deep enough to plumb the bottom of a reservoir lake or reach productive depths over the outside reefs.

One design is that which features a very large added lip of metal or plastic.

The other is a deep, slanted head that acts as a planer. Additional weight inside the lure adds even more depth potential.

193

Sea Hawk

Bagley Divin' B

Sonar

Deep Rebel

Weight alone is not enough to keep a plug running real deep on a troll or a fast retrieve. You can prove this quickly with a heavy lead jig. Though one of the best lures of all for deep-casting with a slow retrieve, even a jig weighing several ounces will rise far off the bottom when you crank it fast, or troll it.

As already hinted, some shallow-running lures are offered in special deep models with much larger lips.

The great majority of deep-running plugs are used by anglers in deep lakes, particularly reservoir lakes. But deep-divers also work beautifully in salt water. They can be counted on to take grouper and snapper over the reefs—tarpon and snook in deep channels; kingfish and other pelagic species offshore.

Deep-diving plugs used in the sea, I repeat, should be beefed-up models with heavy hooks, preferably wired through.

RATTLING PLUGS: Plugs that rattle—usually by virtue of small weights inside a hollow chamber—have become all the rage among both freshwater and saltwater casters. "Rattlers" do not constitute a separate group of plugs; in fact, the majority of popular designs—shallow running, deep-running and topwater—all can be found with rattlers these days. Most anglers think the addition of sound adds greatly to the appeal of a proven plug that is properly used. But sound alone is not likely to produce much, if any, action unless everything else is done right.

SOFT PLASTIC LURES

Here's a subject which not only COULD fill a book of its own but SHOULD fill one. These baits, molded of soft plastic, come in countless shapes, every conceivable shade of color, and any length from two inches up to a foot or longer.

The most familiar sub-types are worms, eels, salamanders (lizards), and crawdads, but just about everything that creeps or swims has been by now modeled in soft plastic. Worms, of course, are by far the most widely used.

Though many worms are ready-rigged with one, two, or three hooks, most really avid worm users prefer to rig their own.

As for rigged worms, they work too, and they sell well enough. But worm specialists just like to rig their own.

Plastic worms long ago assumed a premier position in freshwater fishing and, more recently, have become almost as widely established on the saltwater scene. The use of soft plastic worms and grubs in salt water has thus far been primarily in combination with lead-head jigs. (See the section on "Jigs" for more detail.) However, new uses are being discovered every day. For instance, the plain, unleaded worm has taken tarpon, snook, grouper, snapper and numerous other species. In certain situations it produces nearly as well as natural bait. What situations? The field is so wide open all anglers should do their own experimenting.

Some of the newly-discovered uses of plastic worms are real eyebrow-raisers. Fishermen have used a simple worm on a popping cork rig, instead of shrimp or other natural bait, and have made

Culprit

Jelly Worm

Creme Rigged Crawler

Original Mr. Twister Curl-Tail

Limit Finder

Lizard

Crawfish

hefty catches of trout. Others have drifted worms behind a moving boat, both on the flats and in deeper water, and socked trout, jack, snapper, barracuda, and many other types.

What about color? In fresh water, standard colors for a long time have been black, blue and purple. However, many other hues are in wide use—green, various shades of red, spotted patterns, yellow, amber. Keep several colors on hand. Be guided by local advice, but don't be afraid to vary your colors if fishing is slow.

In salt water, the most popular hues seem to be yellow or chartreuse, white, pink—and orange for tarpon and snook. Also popular at sea is the clear worm, with a phosphorescent finish that glows in the dark. There isn't much light, you know, at depths of 100 feet or more, and the luminous worm does good work down there.

Six inches has long been the one most popular length of worm among bassers, although seven- and eight-inchers are nearly as widely used. Giant models of 10 and 12 inches have ups-and-downs in popularity.

Worms smaller than a half-foot also get much play—and not just for panfish, but for bass. In clear water, or hard-fished areas, four-inch worms often get hits where larger models are ignored.

RIGGING THE WORM

The following rigs work equally well with all elongated plastic baits—not just eels and worms, but also lizards, crawfish and squid-like baits— so long as there is sufficient length and thickness in the forward portion of the lure to accommodate the chosen hook. Any plastic bait that is too short to rig with the hook hidden must, of course, be rigged with the hook exposed.

The original self-rigged worm is shown in the first illustration— a single hook stuck into the worm at the head. This is still a good rig, particularly with six-inch worms and in open water. It can be used without a weight of any kind and allowed to settle slowly or allowed to drift with the current, adding a bit of rod action from time to time. If it must be sent deeper, you add a split shot, perhaps two, immediately in front of the hook. At least one shot is generally used in a lake or other still water, so that the worm can go to bottom and be retrieved slowly, with a stop-and-go technique.

If weeds are a problem, or if the bottom is snaggy, the same rig can be effected simply by substituting a weedless hook for the plain hook.

Weedless hooks, though, have largely lost out in angler esteem to special "worm hooks," designed so that the worm itself serves as a weed guard. Worm hooks have an abrupt bend or angle in the shank, just behind the eye of the hook. They are rigged as shown in the third illustration—only the bent portion of the shank goes into the head of the worm. The rest of the hook stays outside, except for the point and barb, which is pushed up into the worm and left buried.

Weedless rigging can be accomplished in the same way even with hooks of traditional pattern, via the "Texas Rig." The Sproat pattern

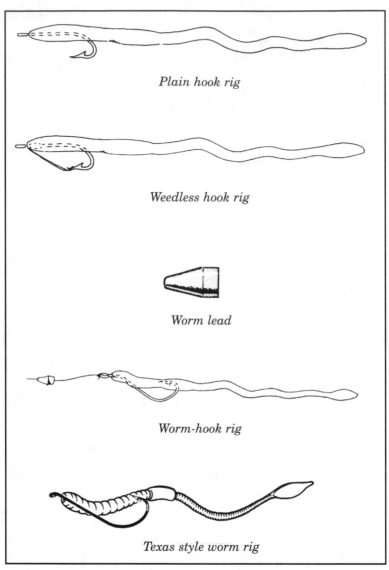

Plain hook rig

Weedless hook rig

Worm lead

Worm-hook rig

Texas style worm rig

is most widely used. Aberdeen hooks work well with Texas rigs when light spinning gear is used, but are not sturdy enough to withstand the pressures of heavy baitcasting lines.

In the Texas Rig, you insert the hook point into the head of the worm and bring it out only a quarter-inch or so below. Then the hook is spun completely around and pulled down so that the hook-eye is buried in the head of the worm. Last, the hook point is inserted into the body of the worm. Since there is no sharp bend on the

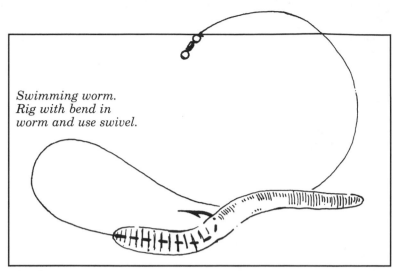

*Swimming worm.
Rig with bend in
worm and use swivel.*

shank to serve as an anchor, it is common practice to insert a round wooden toothpick through the worm and the hook-eye. The toothpick is then trimmed flush with the worm to anchor it.

Various specialty hooks are available for worm-rigging. In some, a U-bend takes the place of the standard hook eye. The short end of the "U" is pointed and barbed, and you simply insert it into the head of the worm, and then affix the hook to the body of the worm in regular fashion. A somewhat similar design does have a regular eye, but attached thereto is a small barbed shaft which you insert into the head of the worm.

With the Texas rig, and most other worm rigs, care is taken to see that the worm lies as straight as possible on the hook to avoid twisting: however, some worm rigs—notably the Carolina rig—are deliberately designed to spin or twist on the retrieve. At times, the spinning worm is definitely more productive. To rig a worm for spinning, you simply position the hook point farther down the worm—an inch or so—and leave a pronounced bend in the worm when the rig is finished. To help avoid line twist, a Carolina rig or spinning worm should be used with a swivel, placed a foot or so above the worm.

Any worm rigged with the hookpoint buried should be used with quite a stiff rod. You have to take up all slack and give a mighty yank to make sure the point goes through the worm and into the fish. This is the reason stiff-action freshwater rods, either baitcasting or spinning, are so often referred to as "worm rods."

WORM LEAD: A special type of sliding sinker called a "worm lead" or "cone lead," is frequently used in combination with the Texas rig and other weedless arrangements. Like the egg sinker of salt water, the worm lead is threaded onto the line, where it slides freely; however, its pointed nose allows it to slither more easily through weeds or among snags. In years past, nearly all bassers allowed the worm lead to slide, but a great many now "peg" the same lead firmly to the line, flush with the head of the worm. Pegging is done by shoving a tapered toothpick into the channel of the sinker as far as possible, then breaking off the toothpick flush with the sinker's head.

The pegged sinker allows better control of the worm during the retrieve—much the same control as with a jig—besides which, hangups are reduced.

Basic system for fishing a plastic worm, rigged or unrigged, is to let it sink to bottom and then wind it slowly back to you with short upward lifts of the rodtip, and pauses between lifts.

But, as with any other kind of fishing, the basic system is not enough by itself. Sometimes the worm produces more strikes if wound steadily through the water at a slow speed. Other times, a medium or even fast retrieve is needed to attract fish.

Not a few fishermen use worms just as they would a plug or other lure. They cast it to the shoreline or cover, retrieve it a few feet in stop-and-go fashion, then wind it in and cast again. These folks feel—and with considerable justification, that bass are going to hit early in the retrieve or not at all.

The weedless-rigged worm is also a sensational lure for fishing in thick grass and lily pads. Toss it out in the jungle, wind slowly and let it snake around weeds or over the top of lily pads. If it hits a small pocket of open water, let it sink a few seconds before starting it on its way again.

As a rule, some dropback, or slack line, should be given when a bass takes the worm. But not much. As soon as you sense fair pressure or any sort of steady pull—hit him!

There really is no standard procedure for timing your strike in worm fishing. When you gain some experience, your intuition probably will take over.

JERK WORMS: This category is relatively new and is made up of lures that are molded of plastic that is soft, yet a bit harder than the usual formula for plastic worms. This, combined with additional thickness of the bait over the forward portion, allows the incorporation of an immensely valuable design feature—a long, open groove in the top surface of the lure. Thus, when you rig in "Texas" fashion, as described earlier, the hookpoint is not left buried in the bait, but rests in the groove. It is fully protected from hangup on limbs and grass, yet does not have to penetrate the bait when a fish strikes.

Jerk baits by different manufacturers have different shapes.

They can be worm-like, slug-like, shiner-like or simply cigar-shaped. But the hook-protecting groove categorizes them, as does the manner in which they are fished: They are generally retrieved slowly, with pauses and occasional jerks. Regardless of individual shape, all seem to simulate a creature in extreme distress, and they have proven to be among the most fish-catching of all lures for bass and coastal predators alike. Their phenomenal success is due in part to the fact that they are the most weedless of lures and can be thrown or retrieved virtually anywhere without hanging up.

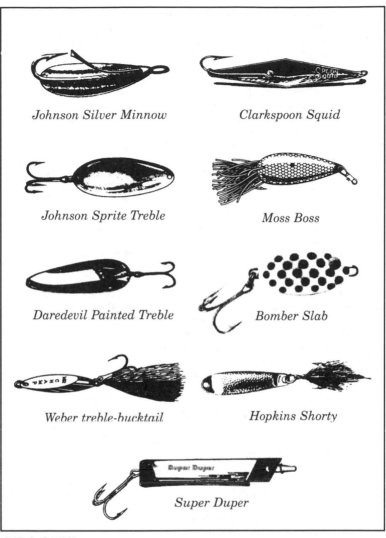

Johnson Silver Minnow

Clarkspoon Squid

Johnson Sprite Treble

Moss Boss

Daredevil Painted Treble

Bomber Slab

Weber treble-bucktail

Hopkins Shorty

Super Duper

SPOONS

Spoons comprise one of the oldest and simplest types of artificial lure in existence, yet they remain perennially popular everywhere—in salt water and fresh water alike.

Though you'll find many slight variations in shape and great variation in color and finish, all spoons work in essentially the same way—their dished-out shape giving them a wobbling or darting motion, and their metallic finish providing flash.

Spoons painted on one side and shiny on the other are frequently used in fresh water, but seldom in coastal fishing. This is nothing but habit; painted spoons do attract saltwater fish. In fact, the saltwater spoon fisherman is in pretty much of a rut. He may use spoons of different sizes and different designs, but he almost always insists on silver ones, with gold reserved for particular applications, such as shallow-water fishing for redfish.

The freshwater man, on the other hand, may often use a painted spoon. He also will probably use silver under bright conditions; gold during an overcast; black on a very dark day or at night.

Treble-hooked spoons are used mostly for casting—either in open fresh waters, particularly for schooling fish like white bass, or in open salt water for such fish as mackerel, blues and trout.

The saltwater fisherman uses many more single-hook spoons than the inland angler, both for casting and trolling. However, a weedless spoon with a single hook is one of the ancient standbys in fresh water for fishing in thick grass, pads, or snaggy shallows.

The freshwater weedless spoon is almost always fitted with a trailer of some sort—a strip of pork rind, a pork-chunk frog, a plastic skirt or a plastic worm.

About 90 percent of the time, a straight retrieve at slow-to-moderate speed gives any spoon its best payoff punch. Faster cranking pays off in salt water when the prey species are fast swimmers like mackerel. And in fresh water, it's a good idea to try holding your rod tip high, cranking fast, and making your spoon skitter along the top of the grass, when fishing in densely weeded water.

Believe it or not, bass can shoulder their way through all kinds of submerged moss and weeds and nail a fast-moving spoon on top of the water. If they do miss, you at least see where they are and can cast to the same spot and try a slower return.

SLAB SPOONS: Designed for "yo-yoing," or vertical retrieving, in deep water, these are metallic lures that differ from other spoon designs in having flattened surfaces rather than dished-out ones. Larger lures of this type that are used in salt water are usually called metallic jigs, rather than slab spoons, (see the section on Jigs, which follows). One or more surfaces of the lure may be painted, or hammered for more reflection. A slab spoon flutters as it sinks and is usually worked by lifting the rod and allowing the spoon to settle back. The strike usually comes while the lure is falling.

See the chapter on "Saltwater Baits and Lures" for tips on trolling a spoon in salt water.

SPINNERS AND SPINNERBAITS

The spinner is another ancient type of fishing lure and comes in many sizes, shapes and forms.

Spinners—again by tradition and not for practical reasons—are used almost entirely in fresh water. But there, one form or another of spinner has proven deadly for taking all types of freshwater fish, from small sunfish and mountain trout to huge largemouth bass, pike and muskies. Many fish in salt water will take spinners, but the lure never has caught on well in the sea.

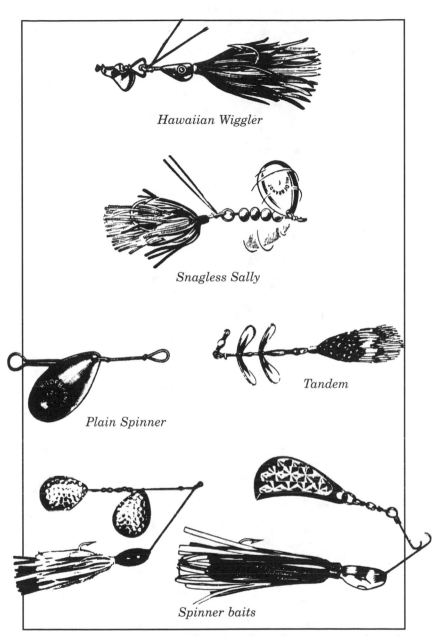

Hawaiian Wiggler

Snagless Sally

Plain Spinner

Tandem

Spinner baits

When you hear the term "spinnerbait," it refers to just one branch of the spinner family—one that challenges plastic worms in the esteem of bass fishermen. In this type lure, a single or double spinner revolves above the dressed hook, in a V-wire configuration that

203

Beetle Spin   *Walleye Spinner*

Mepps   *Panther Martin*

Buzzbait

is reminiscent of an open safety pin, as you can see in the accompanying illustrations. Although not technically "weedless"—at least not in truly dense vegetation—the spinnerbait's very design makes it virtually snag-free in scattered grass, and the lure seldom hangs on hard snags, either. In fact, many experts like to "knock" their spinnerbaits against tree trunks and other woody structure whenever they can during the retrieve, feeling the noise generates impulsive strikes from lurking bass.

The basic retrieve for a spinnerbait is slow and steady, but stop-and-go tactics produce too, and a spinnerbait also is deadly when used much like a jig—with an up-and-down retrieve near bottom in deep water.

Very small spinnerbaits, weighing an eighth of an ounce or less, are killers for crappie and other panfish. Many of these are simply miniature versions of the popular bass baits. Others feature marabou or other crappie jigs on the bottom leg of the "V." Still others—the Beetle Spins, for example, get their appeal from hooks dressed with molded plastic imitations of caterpillars and other insect baits.

BUZZBAITS: These are simply spinnerbaits with large, modified spinners that keep the lure splattering the surface, even on fairly slow retrieves. This concept in fishing has proven very effective in varied water conditions, from deep impoundments to brush lakes and ponds. The buzzbaits are almost weedless, due to the oversize spinner that "walks" over and around weed clumps.

Spinners built on a straight piece of wire, rather than in "V" form, are often called in-line spinners to distinguish them from spinnerbaits.

Among the best-known of in-line spinners are the Rooster Tail, Panther Martin, Bang Tail, Shyster and, of course, the various Mepps lures. Generally, they are small, running from one-sixteenth of an ounce, or even lighter, to a half-ounce. Larger ones are made.

The best all-around sizes are one-eighth and one-quarter ounce, simply because little spinners of that size have no challengers in fresh water for constant action and sheer variety. Panfish love them, and they take a goodly share of bragging-size bass and other fish as well. There are a lot of better lures for large bass, but the lunkers do hit tiny spinners with surprising gusto at times. In addition to bass and bream, spinners regularly take pickerel, crappie (speckled perch), warmouth, northern species of perch, white bass, freshwater trout, and of course, rough fish such as gars and mudfish. In short, anything that feeds on either minnows or insect life is apt to slug a little spinner. Even quite a few catfish have been caught on them.

Of course, there are similar but larger in-line spinners designed for larger fish. Hawaiian Wigglers, for example, were catching big bass for many years before the safety-pin spinnerbaits even came upon the scene—and they are by no means the most venerable of the classic in-line spinners. The Shimmy Wiggler has been around even longer, while one version or another of the Yellow Sally spinner is familiar to several generations of fishermen.

WALLEYE SPINNERS: Like most predatory gamefish, walleyes hit a variety of baits, lures and bait-lure combinations, but are so responsive to a specialized type of in-line spinner that it has come to be widely referred to as a "walleye lure." It's identifying features are that the spinner turns behind a leaded head (in most small spinner-lures, the blade rides in front of the head), and that it almost always wears a single hook instead of the trebles common on general-purpose spinners.

The walleye spinner will catch plenty of fish all by itself, but its single hook usually is dressed up with a live minnow, earthworm or leech. Dead specimens of the same baits are used too, as are plastic imitations.

Now, as always, the fisherman has a huge choice of plain spinners at his command (along with other necessary components) with which to create his own lures. Plain spinners are offered in several styles and many sizes, from small enough to use ahead of trout flies to large enough for custom-made bass and musky lures.

JIGS

In most circles, the word "jig" refers to a single hook, molded into a lead head and dressed with bucktail or other hairs, nylon filaments, feathers, Mylar strips, rubber skirts or any combination of those and similar materials.

It's possible that more anglers—in fresh and salt water combined—get more mileage out of jigs than any other type of artificial lure.

A new jig "material" has been added to the list of dressings in more recent years—soft plastic baits, such as worms, curly-tail worms, grubs, shrimp or crawfish, and squid-like gadgets aplenty. Whether the worm is threaded onto the hook of a bare lead-head, or used as an added attraction for a bucktail or rubber-skirted jig, it does some pretty devastating work on a variety of fish, from inland waters to the deep sea.

Jigs with plastic attractors are often called "baittails." They can be purchased in numerous ready-made forms, or fashioned in tailor-made style by the angler himself. The fisherman who makes his own can instantly create anything from a crappie or bonefish jig to an extra-heavy deep jig—just by threading a worm, or the tail piece of a worm, onto a lead-head of appropriate size.

Of the many plastic tails used with jig heads, one of the best and most popular features a curled, flattened tail which has the most natural swimming motion imaginable. These may be referred to as "twisters"—after the original Mr. Twister tail—or "screw-tails."

Plastic tail styles that have achieved great popularity also include the Mann Grub, Boone Tout and Bagley Salty Dog Shrimp.

Regardless of whether your jigs are dressed with conventional materials, plastic worms, or a combination of both, they are all fished in essentially the same style.

Most fish seem to prefer jigs when they are retrieved near bottom at a slow-to-medium speed. Crank the reel a few times, then twitch the rod to make the jig hop. Continue this pattern to boatside. But, as with all fishing rules, there are numerous exceptions. Fast retrieves sometimes produce better, particularly when going after mackerel or offshore species. And even the kinds of fish which

Cotee Grub

Cotee Weedless Shad

Pompano jig

Skirted, weedless bass jig

Diamond jig

Hopkins

Metallic Jigs

normally prefer a slow, hopping retrieve can often be enticed out of a stubborn streak by changing suddenly from a slow retrieve to a fast one.

And when fishing lakes, you obviously would not hop your jig near bottom when fish are hitting at or near the surface.

How do you select the right jig? It really isn't too difficult a job, despite the hundreds of different jig designs and color variations.

The only consideration that might, of itself, spell success or failure is weight. Select weight according to your tackle and the depth you are trying to reach.

For freshwater fishing, and most inshore saltwater work—such as seatrout over flats, or for fishing along shorelines and around bars—the usual weight range is from one-eighth to one-half ounce. Freshwater bassers tend to stick almost entirely to jigs with thick rubber skirts, usually fitted with a pork chunk to make the lure called "jig-and-pig." Worms or other plastic trailers can be substituted for the pork.

Jigs of lighter weight will frequently prove useful for fish such as crappie, perch and bluegills, or in salt water for moonfish and other panfish. Of course, light weights cannot be used unless your tackle is light enough to toss them.

Nylure nylon jig

Popeye skimmer head

Hurricane bucktail

You'll need some jigs weighing five-eighths or one ounce, for deep-lake fishing; deep-hole coastal fishing; and for offshore and reef fishing in water up to say, 50 feet or so in depth. In water without current, a five-eighth or one-ounce jig can even be used at much greater depth.

Jigs larger than one-ounce in weight are used almost exclusively for deep-jigging offshore in water of around 80 to 150 feet. Such jigs may weigh two or three ounces. Big chunks of lead like that require extra-stout rods to even make them move at such depths.

Another factor in jig selection is color, but not so important as you might think. White and yellow have been standard colors for many years (both inland and in the sea), and you could probably get by very well on these alone. But there are many other popular hues—pink, orange, red, blue, brown and varied mixed patterns.

If you're just getting started, rely mostly on white and yellow. Experiment with a few others on the basis of local advice, and draw your own conclusions.

Now for the matter of dressing. Animal hairs and plastic worms seem to give the most lifelike actions but feathers are not far behind. In fact, Marabou feathers are the wiggliest of all.

On the other hand, nylon is far more durable. A lot of fishermen use bucktail, feather or worm-jigs routinely, but keep nylon jigs handy for mackerel or other species which tear up jigs easily.

Note, however, that an awful lot of anglers use nylon jigs regularly for both light freshwater and saltwater fish, and get consistently good catches. You can see, therefore, that choosing the proper dressing material is not exactly a critical thing.

Only one item of choice remains—head style. Here, except for a

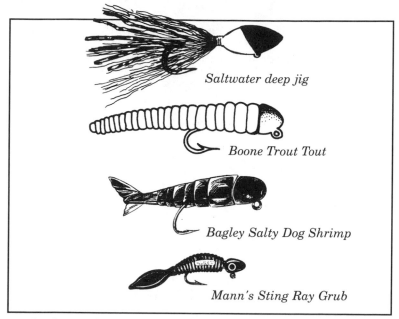

Saltwater deep jig

Boone Trout Tout

Bagley Salty Dog Shrimp

Mann's Sting Ray Grub

couple of specialized purposes, the choice matters hardly a bit.

One such specialized head is the style known in saltwater circles as a "skimmer," and in freshwater areas as a "glider." These have heads which are flattened horizontally, and sometimes slightly dished out. When retrieved, they plane upward in the water, hence the name "skimmer." They are preferred by bonefishermen, and other saltwater folks who fish very shallow flats.

Lake fishermen use the same type head for a different purpose. They allow it to sink slowly in deeper water. As it sinks it wobbles or "glides" with very enticing action—hence the other name, "glider."

Another specialty head is the one that is flattened vertically rather than horizontally. This design, commonly seen in the Cotee line, among many others, tends to dart or wobble during the descent than jigs of the same weight, but with blunt or rounded heads, which sink straighter and faster.

For all-around use in shallow and medium depths, you'll find votes for bullet-shaped heads, round heads, lima-bean-shaped heads, and others. Every style has its staunch followers and there is no way to determine which is "best."

Success with any jig, in any water, depends far more on how much you cast, and how much you experiment with retrieves than it does on design, color or anything else.

Pick a weight that's suited to your tackle and water conditions, and you're in promising shape.

METALLIC JIGS: Heavy, spoon-like lures designed to sink fast so that they can be jigged vertically (although they are also trolled, or cast in the surf) wear the name of jigs in certain coastal areas. Some types are called squids or diamond jigs. Hopkins and Bead Chain are among popular brands. Most metallic saltwater jigs are heavy, weighing from one ounce to several ounces, and are best used with stout rods. Smaller versions of this type lure are used for inshore casting, and also used in fresh water, where they usually are referred to as "slab spoons."

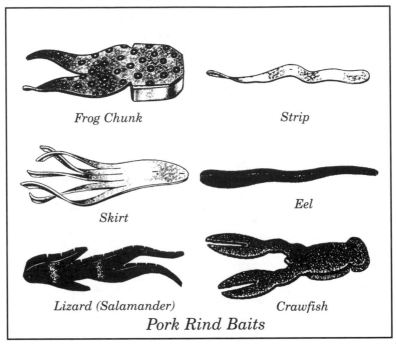

Frog Chunk

Strip

Skirt

Eel

Lizard (Salamander)

Crawfish

Pork Rind Baits

PORK RIND BAITS

Strips and chunks of pork rind have been used by fishermen far longer than have their plastic counterpart. Nowadays it seems as if the pork comes in almost as many variations.

While pork baits are perhaps most widely employed as trailers tacked onto other lures, such as spoons, spinners and jigs, many are also excellent producers of fish when allowed to perform solo. Pork eels, for example, were predecessors of plastic eels as "revolutionary" bass baits. Stuck to a weedless hook and snaked slowly along bottom, or through pads, weeds and grass, the "eelbait" as it came to be called in the 1950s, would frequently clobber bass when they could not be caught on the standard hard lures. They remain just as productive, of course, even though the plastic eels and worms that came along at the height of the "eelbait's" popularity, stole away the limelight.

The advantage of plastic eels is that they do not have to be stored in brine when not being fished. On the other hand, plastic baits are many times less durable.

Pork frogs also can be killers when fished in and around pads on weedless hooks.

In saltwater, large pork rind strips take many species of fish, from stripers and blues up to billfish—whether rigged to a pinned hook in the fashion of a saltwater fish strip, or used as a trailer with jigs and trolling feathers.

Pork strips come in all sizes, from an inch to 10 inches, and every one has great appeal to fish of appropriate size. Pork also comes in various shapes, of which the pork frog is probably the most familiar.

One of the best-known—and most productive—combination baits in all of freshwater fishing is a weedless spoon with a pork rind trailer. The trailer is usually a strip when the angler wants an underwater retrieve, and a frog when he wants to keep his lure on or near the top of the water.

FLIES AND FLYROD LURES

It's hard to imagine, but there are many more variations in flies and flyrod lures than even in plugs or jigs or other kinds of artificials.

That's because for every one of the hundreds of different patterns and models offered by large suppliers, there are hundreds more variations made by small commercial tiers, or by individuals.

Many ponderous books have been written about fly patterns. We can only concern ourselves here with a look at the various categories of flies and flyrod lures, for familiarization.

Local advice is always of strong importance when selecting flies—particularly for freshwater trout fishing, but also for bass and panfishing, and saltwater fishing.

DRY FLIES—Dries are used in fresh water only, and can be identified by the very heavy hackling that allows them to float on the surface. Even so, they must be dressed to assure high floating qualities over extended periods. The dry fly user also false casts several times between actual casts to dry the fly. Dries are cast upcurrent, and must be allowed to float for as long a distance as possible without line drag.

In trout fishing, it is often important to imitate—or at least strongly suggest—common insects of the particular locality when selecting dry fly patterns, especially if a "hatch" of insects is taking place.

Bream and other panfish take dry flies readily and often are not at all selective as to pattern.

WET FLIES are flies that do not float, but which are allowed to drift under the surface, usually near the top. Like dry flies, they are tied to imitate or suggest certain natural flies. Wets generally are cast across the current, or slightly upstream, and allowed a long natural down-stream drift. The fisherman may strip line or twitch the rodtip to provide extra action at the end of the drift.

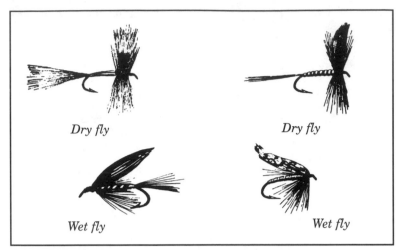

Dry fly　　　　　　　　　*Dry fly*

Wet fly　　　　　　　　　*Wet fly*

Again, bluegills and other panfish take wet flies without nearly as much selectivity as is often displayed by wild trout.

STREAMER FLIES are also fished "wet" but are made to imitate minnows instead of insects. Though they can often be drifted with good effect, they are usually stripped in with short jerks, either across the current or upcurrent. In calm water, such as lakes or bays, streamers are always stripped in to imitate the erratic darting action of a small fish.

Most bass flies and saltwater flies are streamers of large size.

Probably the most widely familiar streamer of all is the Muddler—tied in a variety of sizes and deadly on all types of freshwater predatory fish from small trout to big bass.

Bass incidentally, are great streamer-fly fish. Bass streamers are mostly tied on hooks of No. 4 to No. 2/0 in size. Trout streamers generally are No. 10, 8, 6, sometimes smaller.

In the South, fly fishermen who go after bass use mostly popping bugs. Many who use popping bugs exclusively would be pleasantly surprised to see how streamers pay off many times when poppers aren't inducing any strikes at all.

NYMPHS are similar in usage to wet flies. However, they are tied to imitate the immature, or nymphal, stage of an insect rather than the adult, winged stage, and usually are fished deeper—often by tumbling them right along the bottom. Obviously, some weight may be needed to accomplish this presentation. The nymph itself may be a weighted tie, or a bit of lead can be added to the leader. Most nymphs are tied without wings though there are tiny wings on some. Generally, they are tied for body conformation, perhaps with material to suggest legs.

Used almost entirely by trout fishermen, nymphs take panfish well in rivers and creeks. Local advice is vital in nymph selection.

MOLDED FLYROD LURES cover a wide range of actual molded imitations, in plastic, of nymphs, grubs, caterpillars, hellgrammites, spiders, crickets, grasshoppers etc. A well-known example is the molded mayfly nymph so popular for bream and bass in southern waters. Trout anglers generally shun the molded imitations, but they are dear to the hearts of panfishermen everywhere.

FLYROD "HARD" LURES include tiny plugs, spoons and spinners, made much like their larger spinning-lure counterparts. They are not overly popular among fly fishermen—except for the little spinners, which often are used in combination with wet flies, or with natural bait, such as worms.

SALTWATER FLIES, as mentioned, are usually large streamers tied either with animal hair, or with long feathers (hackle). A recent, and very good, trend has been to include a few strips of shiny Mylar in most all of the saltwater flies. In addition to streamers, saltwater flies designed for bonefish and permit are tied to imitate shrimp or small crabs. Flies with epoxy heads have become popular on the flats because they dive to bottom quickly and can be

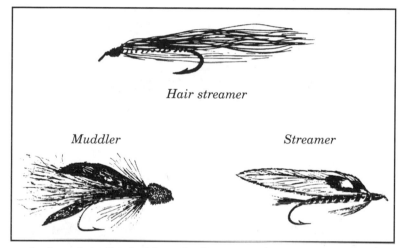

Hair streamer

Muddler   *Streamer*

worked much in the fashion of a jig.

Streamers for light saltwater use—small striped bass, snook, seatrout, small tarpon, jack, ladyfish and other coastal varieties, should be up to about three inches in overall length, with a hook size of 1/0 to 3/0. Plain yellow, or plain white, in either hair or feather, are good producers. Mylar strips definitely help. There isn't a great deal of variation in pattern, but a wide choice in color combination. A streak of red, blue or black, helps in a white streamer. Red-and-yellow combinations are popular.

For all practical purposes, tarpon flies, offshore flies and other flies for big saltwater fish are merely enlarged versions of the coastal flies. They may have an overall length of up to six inches, and a hook up to 5/0 or 6/0, occasionally larger.

The most popular tarpon fly is a breathing feather streamer in yellow, orange, yellow-orange combination, or grizzly.

213

Molded mayfly nymph

Molded cricket

Nymphs

Flyrod plug

Saltwater streamer

Multi-wing streamer

Bonefish fly

Bonefish shrimp fly

Among the most common offshore patterns for billfish and big dolphin is a large, white fly tied with a dozen or more long hackles, interspersed with strips of Mylar.

As with freshwater fly fishing, it always pays to check for local preferences. Knowledgeable saltwater fly fishermen, guides and shop personnel are no longer hard to find, not even in many areas far removed from the saltwater grounds.

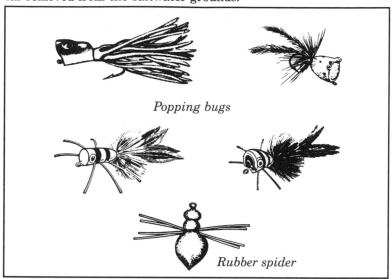

Popping bugs

Rubber spider

POPPING BUGS are the flyrodder's equivalent of surface plugs. They float atop the water and are made to pop by twitching the rod upward. Only occasionally are they used by trout fishermen, but are standards for panfish and for bass. They are often used in saltwater too—in special ties, of course, with saltwater hooks.

Panfish poppers range from tiny things, as small as No. 10, to perhaps as large as No. 4. Bass poppers are usually found in the No. 4 to No. 2/0 size range, with Nos. 2, 1 and 1/0 being perhaps the most widely used. (Sizes refer to hook sizes.)

Popping bugs are made of cork, balsa, or hollow plastic, dressed with feather or hair "tails." A lot of them have rubber legs as well.

They should be fished slowly—popped, then allowed to rest. Faster retrieves may pay off at times, and are best accomplished with bugs that have bullet-shaped rather than popping heads. These are called "sliders" because they skim across the top without digging in and, of course, make less noise. They should be tried if the loud poppers don't work.

There are also hair bugs, made entirely of tightly-twisted or tied bucktail. These too ride the surface with little commotion and are deadly when fish seem spooky.

Another very popular type of floating "bug" is the sponge rubber spider with rubber legs—one of the best-liked of all bream lures.

Chapter 10

Baits, Rigs & Tackle

Angling Accessories

Although the proper tackle, rigs and baits are at the heart of consistently successful fishing, the well-equipped angler relies on many accessory items as well. These range from such things as tackle boxes and bait containers—obvious and important fishing equipment—down to such supplies as insect repellent and fingernail clippers, which are easily overlooked or forgotten, but for which you would sometimes pay any price when you suddenly need them and don't have them on hand.

Some accessory gear is common to nearly all fishermen—nets, knives, coolers. Others must be chosen with particular types of angling in mind. A trout fisherman certainly doesn't need a flying gaff, and a tuna fisherman has little use for a fish stringer.

A wide range of accessories is described in this chapter, but there are many other useful items available to the angler. That's all to the good. It gives you a chance to spend additional hours browsing in your favorite tackle store or department, or through mail order catalogs.

172 Qt., divided lid.

80 Qt., Bottles in lid.

Steel Chest

40 Qt.

Foam

ICE CHESTS OR COOLERS

A warm-weather fisherman's best friend is his cooler. One or more ice chests aboard a boat assures you of bringing home fish that are in peak table condition, and at the same time keeps a cooling drink close at hand when the sun is beating down.

Like tackle boxes, coolers come in a great variety of sizes, from six-pack size to gigantic. Most are made of hard plastic or foam, but steel chests are also offered. A saltwater angler wouldn't go for the steel, but it would make sense for many freshwater fishermen, especially those who camp and need a little more security against hungry wildlife, such as raccoons or bears.

In making a selection, one good approach is to compromise on size and get the largest capacity which you can easily handle in transporting from home to car to boat. Certainly the most popular size range among fishermen is 40 to 50 quarts. Chests up to 60 quarts or so are marginal for one-man carrying, and larger coolers are two-man loads.

Medium or large coolers may well serve as repository for both catch and drinks. Mixing fish with drinks will require that you carefully clean the bottle before you drink, but that's a small price to pay for convenience. Some models have divided compartments. A particularly good arrangement is one in which the dividers are flat plastic water bottles that fit into grooves on the inside of the chest.

On the other hand, if you have plenty of room, a large box for the catch (or the bait and the catch) plus a smaller one for drinks and lunch is a welcome combination.

There is no better way to handle any fish you plan to eat than to deposit them directly on ice. Even stringers do not preserve freshness nearly so well. Keep the fish whole on ice until you clean them. After cleaning, fish should be placed in plastic bags or other watertight containers before going back into the cooler. Dressed fish should not be allowed to come into contact with water, even that which has recently melted from ice.

Though most modern ice chests are very good, there is some variation in cold-keeping ability. One ingenious method of increasing the life of ice is found in Rubbermaid's Gott line of coolers, some of which have flat plastic bottles which are fastened to the inside of the lid. When filled with water and frozen, the bottles provide all the cold needed for prechilled items or for very short outings. When ice is in the box, they extend its thawing time greatly.

Inexpensive—often dirt cheap, in fact—foam ice chests are widely available in many sizes. They are very efficient, especially if the lid can be pressed or sealed tightly, but are too fragile for general angling use. Still, they can be valuable in a pinch, or for such uses as transporting fish and bait for long distances in a car.

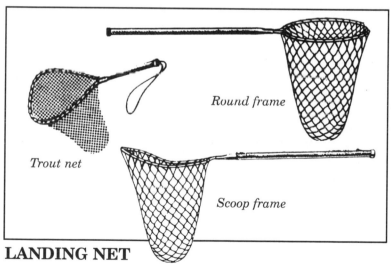

Round frame

Trout net

Scoop frame

LANDING NET

Most present-day landing nets have aluminum handles and framing, with mesh of nylon, plastic or, in some cases, rubber. Cotton mesh nets are available, but will weaken or rot, especially in saltwater use. Nylon nets do not cost that much more.

While diameter of the hoop and length of the handle vary widely,

219

it's a good idea to use as large a net as you can comfortably handle and easily stow. A net with a three-to-four-foot handle, and a hoop diameter of 18-24 inches will serve most purposes.

Special long-handled nets can be found if you fish, say, from docks or seawalls. But for fishing from structures higher than a few feet (many ocean piers and many bridges), the only practical landing net to use is a large hoop net lowered by a rope. These specialized nets are provided at many piers and some fishermen carry them to bridges. A more common device for landing fish from bridges, however, is the bridge gaff, described in the section on gaffs.

With the ordinary landing net, scoop up your fish with a quick motion, but not a wild splashing one. If possible, put the net in the water, lead the fish close to it, and net him with a fast sweeping motion, head first. If you touch a fish's tail with the net, he'll scoot away.

Check nets often for rips or tears, and repair even small holes by tying the mesh with nylon or Dacron line, or even monofilament line. Small holes quickly become big ones.

4-inch hook

2-inch hook

GAFFS

Although a net serves most landing needs for the freshwater and inshore saltwater fisherman, anyone who fishes the reefs or offshore waters should definitely have a gaff aboard. Even inshore you're likely to need a gaff from time to time in order to handle a catch too large to get in your net. Should such a happy occasion arise, you'll be very glad indeed you have a gaff.

Best all-around gaff for light use is one with a stainless steel, two-inch hook—that is, the distance from the point straight across to shaft is two inches. A three or four-foot handle is long enough for most small boats. For boats with high transoms, a six or eight-foot handle may be needed.

The two-inch hook is preferred for small-game fishing because it

220

can be difficult to stick a fish like a school king mackerel or school dolphin with a larger hook. At the same time, however, the two-incher is satisfactory for much larger catches.

If you do a lot of offshore fishing though, it would be wise to complement the two-inch gaff with another, larger one—say a four-incher.

To use a gaff, lower the hook into the water under the fish, then tug smoothly upward to drive the point home. The fish should be hoisted up and into the boat with as little interruption of motion as you can manage, for many fish are adept at tearing loose from a gaff.

Specialty gaffs are made for a variety of purposes, and can be highly useful, or downright essential, depending on your own fishing activities. Let's look at some of them:

FLYING GAFF

Used mostly by big-game fishermen, but occasionally by inshore anglers who go after sharks, the flying gaff features a separate handle and hook. These are fitted together with a temporary fastening, usually light line.

When the gaff hook is driven into a fish, the temporary tie gives way and the hook comes loose from the handle.

Of course, there is a stout rope tied to an eye in the hook, and the other end of the rope is secured firmly to a cleat on the boat.

Once a fish is on the flying gaff, the handle is set aside.

The point of the flying gaff is flattened, sharpened and barbed—all the better to penetrate the tough hide of a big fish, and to resist pulling out once it has been buried.

The flying gaff is used less and less these days as emphasis continues to shift from killing marlin and other big-game fish to releasing them.

RELEASE GAFF

A release gaff is nothing more than a small gaff hook with a very short handle—just large enough to hold in one hand. Some release gaffs have no handle at all—just a loop of rope which is slipped around the gaffer's wrist. The loop, of course, must be large enough so that you can slip out of it instantly if the situation requires.

The release gaff is used mainly on tarpon (of all sizes) which you want to release, while doing the fish as little harm as possible. It can be used, however, for many other large fish that you plan to release.

Play the fish until he is thoroughly whipped. Once he is beside the boat and inactive, you slip the small gaff hook into his mouth and bring the point through his lower jaw. Now you can hold him while you remove the hook, or cut the leader.

SURF GAFF OR "PICK"

The surf gaff is pretty much the same as a release gaff, except that it might have a larger hook bent at a wider angle. It is worn at the belt by surf fishermen. When they hook and whip a large fish that they wish to keep, such as a channel bass or striped bass, they gaff him around the head or "shoulders," and use the short-handled gaff to drag him up the beach.

BRIDGE GAFF

The bridge gaff is nothing more than a large gang-hook (usually a 10/0 size, or larger) which has a hefty chunk of lead molded around the hook shanks.

Since many bridges are too high to permit use of a conventional gaff with a conventional handle, the bridge gaff is used because it works well and can be easily stowed in a bridge-fisherman's kit.

The bridge gaff is tied to a stout line—usually nylon cord. After a fish is whipped and lying on its side below, the fisherman snaps an ordinary shower-curtain ring around both his fishing line and the gaff cord. Then he lowers the gaff.

The shower-curtain ring serves as a guide to steer the gaff to the fish's head. And the ring is large enough so that it can slip over any swivel or other terminal tackle on the fishing line.

The angler may have to do a bit of jiggling with either or both lines to make sure the gaff slides all the way into position.

Once the gang hook is at the fish's head, the angler jerks the cord until the hook takes hold, then handlines his fish up to the catwalk.

Chain stringer, swiveled

Cord stringer

FISH STRINGERS

The two common types of fish stringers are the ordinary cord stringer, and the chain stringer with individual fish clips.

Made of cotton, nylon or twisted plastic, the cord stringer is fitted with a metal point at one end, a metal ring at the other. This type is used principally for panfish, but can be used for larger fish as well. You run the point under the fish's gill cover and out its mouth.

223

Then you run the point through the metal ring. With all the fish after the first, you simply run the point in the gill and out the mouth, sliding the fish to the bottom of the string.

The chain stringers feature safety-pin type clips, usually of spring metal wire, but sometimes of nylon. Favored by bass fishermen, this type stringer is used by opening the "safety pin" and running the point through both lips of the fish. The pin is then snapped shut.

Cord stringers can be obtained in various lengths. The usual is six feet, for use when fishing from a skiff or from shore. Longer ones—sometimes much longer—may be needed by bridge or dock fishermen.

Most freshwater fish and some saltwater species will stay alive for hours if kept on a stringer in the water—that is, if they are not injured beforehand.

Side cutters

Long-nose

Multi-purpose

FISHERMAN'S PLIERS

Wire-cutting pliers are just about a must for saltwater fishermen, and not much less useful to the freshwater fan—because they clip monofilament line and leader, as well as wire.

You have your choice of two basic styles. One is a saltwater standard—the blunt-nosed, square-jaw type with the cutters on the outside. With this style, you can cut wire much easier and faster.

The other is the long-nose type, with the cutters at the base of the jaws. This kind is somewhat more unhandy when it comes to clipping wire, but it does clip efficiently—and its long jaws are often a big help in removing hooks from a fish's gullet.

There are also some long-nosed pliers which feature additional accessories—such as a bottle opener, or perhaps even an adjustable wrench in the handle.

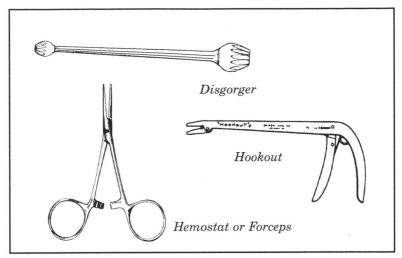

Disgorger

Hookout

Hemostat or Forceps

HOOK REMOVERS

Removing hooks from the mouths of fish can be almost as difficult as getting them there. It should be done routinely with a tool rather than the bare hands, because it can be a dangerous procedure for the fisherman and a delicate one for the fish—especially a fish that you want to release uninjured.

The job becomes even trickier, of course, when the hook is well inside the fish's mouth or throat.

The fisherman's pliers already discussed make pretty good removers—the long-nose styles more so than the snub-nosed type. Numerous single-purpose removers can also be found on tackle counters.

The cheapest device is a plastic disgorger with a small, grooved head at one end and a larger grooved head at the other. Each head is also fitted with a slit for your line. You choose the large or small head—according to which one best accommodates the size of your hook—then place your line in the slit and let the disgorger follow your line down until one of its grooves comes to rest at the bend of the hook. A firm push should then dislodge it. Once free, the hook is protected by the groove so you can ease both line and disgorger out of the fish's mouth together.

Another and more elaborate device features a set of metal-toothed pincers at the end of a long neck. The pincers, operated remotely by your grip, grab the hook firmly so that it can be worked free.

Very small hooks, like those on most freshwater flies, are best attacked with forceps or hemostats, similar (if not identical) to those used by physicians. They are available in nearly all flyfishing supply houses and many general tackle shops and departments.

Quite a few other gadgets for removing hooks (and gripping fish) will vie for your attention in the tackle shops.

225

Pocket model

Heavy duty

LINE CLIPPERS

The familiar pair of fingernail clippers is one of the handiest gadgets an angler can use. No tool is better for clipping line.

Some brands of this type clipper are designed especially for fishermen, and may feature additional accessories—such as a cord for looping to a buttonhole, and a blunted needle for clearing hook-eyes or picking out tangles.

However, the accessories aren't used nearly so often as are the clippers themselves, and for all practical purposes the ordinary fingernail clippers from the drug counter do just as well.

CAUTION: Never attempt to clip wire of any kind with fingernail clippers. You'll only blunt the edges and ruin them.

KNIVES

It would take a whole book just to list the different models of knives offered for sale to fishermen. We'll content ourselves here with a general discussion.

Though it hasn't always been so, you can now get numerous brands of knives with stainless steel blades that take and hold a very keen edge. Only a few anglers still prefer carbon steel knives, which are less expensive and easy to sharpen, but which rust quickly.

As an all-around fisherman's knife, I nominate the fillet-type which has a thin but sturdy blade of stainless steel, and a blade length of six inches. Several of these come with sheaths, which protect the blade when stowed in a tackle box, and which can be worn at your belt while fishing.

Such a knife does a great job of filleting fish, cutting bait, or making rigged baits.

The stainless steel blade has this additional advantage: It can

Stainless fillet Knife

Bait Knife

Folding fillet Knife

Electric Knife

be cleaned up spick and span in a minute, and used for preparing your lunch!

Panfishermen, might find the six-inch blade too large for convenient dressing of stream trout or a mess of bream. Smaller models of the standard curved-blade fillet knives are available for this job, but a good, sharp pocket knife works as well as any.

Charterboat mates and others who make lots of rigged baits may also prefer a tool of paring-knife size. Small bait knives with good, sharp steel are available, so look for those over similar cheapies that have soft plastic handles and dull blades to match.

The industrial age has come to fishing knives as well. Electric knives make quick work of filleting and skinning, and are invaluable when cleaning limit catches of panfish. They are so popular nowadays that many cleaning stations at fish camps offer plug-in sockets for electric knives.

Also available are portable electric knives that you can hitch up to a boat or car battery when AC current is nowhere to be found.

The various "gadget" knives for fishermen—such as folding knives with bottle-openers, scaling edges, etc.—should be selected by the individual for whatever appeal or value they might have to him.

KNIFE AND HOOK SHARPENERS

Every angler's tackle box should contain a sharpening tool—both for his knife and for his hooks.

A small whetstone will do a pretty good job of both. But it isn't a bad idea to carry a larger stone for the knife (it's faster and easier), and either a small stone or a small file for putting a keen point on hooks.

Modern anglers have still other choices—battery-powered sharpeners that are portable enough to fit in a tackle box.

With light-wire freshwater hooks such as the Aberdeen pattern, it may be easier, and not expensive, to change hooks when the point

File with handle

Pocket sharpener

Power hook sharpener

Guided knife sharpener

gets dull or blunted.

The majority of saltwater hooks, even new ones, can do with a bit of sharpening. Being thicker, these hooks are harder to set in a fish. Just a lick or two with hone or file might well save you a trophy fish.

LUBRICANTS

Always carry oil with you when fishing. The level wind mechanism of a revolving spool casting reel should be oiled once or twice during a fishing day for peak performance. And it never hurts, either to drop a bit of oil on both moving ends of a spinning reel bail sometime during the day.

Heavier grease is seldom necessary during an actual fishing trip—since this type lubricant is used mainly inside a reel on the gears.

By far the most useful and versatile of lubricants are the sprays which come in aerosol cans. I strongly recommend carrying a can in the tackle box. If you have a small box, you can buy a small can, but the larger sizes are more economical.

Spray the stuff lightly over all of your reels. It lubricates the external moving parts mentioned above, and also protects your reel from salt spray. The stuff doesn't harm your fishing line.

Don't hesitate to spray anything you wish to protect from corrosion or exposure to salt—rods, reel seats, tackle box hinges, boat hardware, battery terminals, zippers, outboard motors.

These sprays displace moisture and improve electrical contacts, in addition to fighting corrosion.

Be sure to spray your reels, reel seats and rod guides after fishing. Also spray hooks and lures before returning them to your tackle box.

INSECT REPELLENTS

An item often overlooked by an angler—and sometimes to his great pain and suffering—is insect repellent.

If you can't spare the space in your tackle box for a spray-can, you can at least carry a small bottle of repellent lotion, or a stick.

Don't run the risk of being caught without protection from insect bites just because you "don't think" bugs will be a problem in a particular place or a particular season.

The most effective repellents are those containing "Deet"—a civilized way of saying "N-N-Diethyl-M-Toluamide"—and the more the better. Concentrations as high as 100 percent are available, most in lotion form. Aerosol sprays typically contain from about 15 percent to about 40 percent, but some are all Deet. The lighter concentrations are, basically, more pleasant to use if the insect problem is mild. But you won't complain about the stronger solutions when the bugs attack in clouds. Since many insects can bite through clothing, the sprays are the most effective form of repellent, but sticks and small bottles are, of course, handier, and can be easily kept in a tackle box to prevent getting caught short. In addition, they are better for exposed skin because of higher Deet concentrations. Other packs available include roll-ons and treated wipes.

Deet, unfortunately, also can damage certain finishes. Be sure to wipe the palms of your hands as clean as possible after applying the repellent. And avoid spilling it on plastics and varnish finishes.

Some repellents are citronella-based, or even cosmetic based! These do help, and may be preferred if you have any problems with Deet products.

Aerosol spray

Pump spray

Lotion

Stick

Three-tray box   *Drawer box*

TACKLE BOXES

Tackle boxes come in an endless array of sizes, shapes, makeups and material.

Every angler must select his own to fill his particular needs. Here are some general observations:

Plastic boxes are by far the best for saltwater use. Wooden boxes are good, but expensive and heavy.

Aluminum boxes are excellent for freshwater fishermen because they are both strong and light.

If you fish often from small boats where space is at a premium, you might consider relying on two or more small tackle boxes rather than a single large one. Big boxes can be difficult to open in limited space. They also can be difficult to lift or carry as one gets older!

Small divided boxes of clear plastic are useful to everyone. They can be used to sort small items inside a larger box, and also serve as pocket tackle boxes when you wade or bank-fish.

Plastic dividers in most new tackle boxes are resistant to the corrosive effects of plastic worms. Some of the older plastics are not. In any event, it's a good idea to get one or more "worm boxes"—special small plastic boxes with long compartments—which are not harmed by contact with plastic worms. Carry these inside your regular tackle box.

Many anglers prefer "soft" tackle boxes—boxes made of fabric rather than hard plastic. Like other utility bags, these offer a variety of pocket setups. Lures, hooks and other tackle can be stowed inside the bags in small, divided boxes, while other compartments handle reels and additional items of gear.

Cotton fisherman's glove

Rapala cleaning glove

GLOVES

Gloves can be helpful to fishermen in several ways, in addition to the obvious one of keeping his hands warm and functional when the weather gets cold.

In salt water, heavy-duty gloves are vital when fishing offshore; frequently useful for inshore fishing as well.

Always wear gloves when handling a wire leader as you lead a fish in for releasing or gaffing. Even if the leader is monofilament, gloves might save a burn.

Caution dictates that you should wear gloves when gaffing a fish, whether you handle the leader or not. Although many experienced fishermen do the job barehanded, they will probably pay in blood or blisters sooner or later. The same goes for handling any fish with teeth, sharp gills or dorsal spines. Again many experienced folks don't take the trouble to put on gloves. It's something like ignoring the seat belt in your car—999 times out of 1,000 there's no harm done. But that thousandth time—oh boy!

A great many private boaters now seek sailfish, and they often get them. Gloves are essential for proper boating, or even releasing of a sail. You should not use a gaff, but should take the leader in gloved hands and carefully pull the sail close enough so you can get both gloved hands around his bill. Then you either pull him aboard and clobber him, or else cut the leader and let him go.

Cut-proof gloves, worn while filleting fish, will also save a lot of wounds.

Casting gloves, same as golf gloves, are used by some anglers to protect their hands. These are fingerless.

Various offerings in cold-weather gloves—some of neoprene; some of fabrics; also feature freedom for line-handling fingers.

231

Snap-on style

Adjustable belt style

Standup belt

ROD BELTS

In saltwater fishing you may be called upon to fight a fish for many minutes, an hour, maybe two hours or more. Unless you have a rod belt with a socket in which to rest the rod butt, you'll end up with a very sore tummy indeed.

This goes for light, one-hand tackle as well as for a heavy ocean rod.

If you do not use rods with gimbal butts, you'll need only a leather rod belt with leather cup or socket.

For gimbal butts, you need a gimbal belt—that is, a deep socket fitted with a pin, and usually on a swiveling or semi-swiveling mount. The pin, of course, fits into the gimbal slot of your rod butt, and helps you keep the rod upright as you do battle.

Rod belts of special design are needed for Standup fishing (see chapter one). They feature sockets backed by wide, strong plates that prevent even the slightest pressure on the angler's body. They also ride lower than conventional belts, generally over the crotch or upper thigh.

Shoulder harness

Kidney harness

Fish Connection standup harness and belt

Sanyo seat harness

ROD HARNESSES

Harnesses help considerably during long fights with ocean tackle, and are essential for big-game fishing—marlin, giant tuna, deep-fighting of big amberjack or grouper, shark fishing.

Without a harness, you must support the weight of the rod, and apply fighting pressure, with your arms alone. Nobody's arms can stand the strain of this, except with light classes of tackle.

With a harness, you can let your shoulders or back do the hard work, and can even drop your arms to your sides for brief rest periods.

One type of harness is the traditional shoulder harness, made of leather or of heavy canvas with leather straps. You put this on as you would a vest. Two straps in front of you are clipped to the harness rings of your ocean reel. The rod butt, of course, rests either in your gimbal belt, if standing, or in the gimbal of your fishing chair, if seated. The other type of harness is the kidney, seat or back harness, which is used in conjunction with a fighting chair.

There's a big difference between a "fishing chair," mentioned

233

above, and a "fighting chair." The former can be any kind of light, usually swiveling, chair that's fitted with a gimbal. A fighting chair is a massive and complex piece of boat furniture that has an adjustable or removable backrest and a sturdy, adjustable footrest.

The ends of a seat belt, are connected to the reel rings by means of heavy ropes or straps and metal snaps.

Often the harness is made with an integral padded seat, on which the angler sits, but a chair belt may be just a heavily padded belt that rides around the angler's lower back. The seat is a fine touch because it keeps the harness from "riding up" the angler's back while he's fighting his big-game fish.

Harnesses for Standup fishing are similar to the old shoulder harnesses, but only superficially so. The best ones cradle the angler's entire back so there are no weak points to torture his shoulders or other specific places in the anatomy.

In essence, a good Standup harness combines the best advantages of a shoulder harness and a fighting-chair harness.

POLARIZING SUNGLASSES

Any good sunglass contributes to your comfort while fishing but only those with polarizing lenses cut out enough glare to allow you to see much under the surface of the water.

Without polarizing glasses, the bonefisherman might as well stay home. Many other fish are also hunted by sight on the flats, and polarizing glasses are equally essential for all of them.

Even if you don't fish the flats, you would do well to wear polarizing glasses as a matter of routine. In any kind of water, fresh or salt, they'll improve your vision in regard to such things as picking out underwater limbs; distinguishing the wakes of fish from wind ripples; or studying the bottom conditions in reasonably

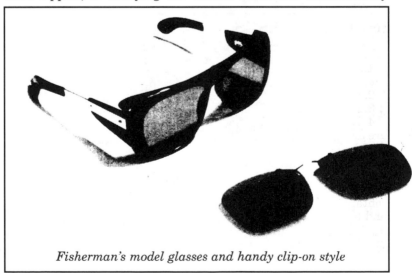

Fisherman's model glasses and handy clip-on style

shallow water.

You also might see a lot of fish in fairly deep water that you might miss if not wearing the glasses.

In case you are confused by terminology, the words "Polaroid" and "polarizing" mean essentially the same thing. "Polaroid" is a brand name and is capitalized. "Polarizing" is a generic term, used for all glasses of this type.

Portable aerator

BAIT BUCKETS AND BOXES

The simplest bait buckets are merely containers which hold water, and which have lids to keep the bait from jumping out. But to hold bait for any length of time, or in any quantity, provisions must be made to replenish the available oxygen supply in the water.

Buckets made of papier-mache or plastic foam hold the oxygen supply better and longer than metal or solid plastic buckets.

To assure an oxygen supply in any container, however, you should take one or more of the following steps:

1. Use O-Tabs, a commercial product which releases oxygen into the water.

2. Change water at frequent intervals, if possible.

3. Keep water cool and shaded. Adding chunks of ice can help.

4. Best of all, use a small pump or aerator. Some very good ones are available at low cost. They clip to the side of the bucket and run on flashlight batteries. For big bait containers, there are heavy duty aerators which connect to the battery of a boat.

Two-piece buckets are popular. These have an inner, perforated container, in which the bait is kept. The inner container is removed and held in the water on a heavy cord. To transport bait, you simply fill the outer bucket with water and place the inner container into it.

There are one-piece buckets which do a similar job. These hold

One-piece trolling bucket

Two piece bucket   *Fiber bucket*

Belt box

Cricket or caterpillar cage

enough water in the bottom to transport bait. But they have perforations at the top, so that when the bucket is lowered by cord from boat or bridge, water freely circulates and keeps the bait frisky.

Some live baits, of course, do not require water at all. Crickets and grasshoppers are kept in light cages of wire or plastic mesh. Some are bucket-shaped with a handle for carrying. Others are tube-shaped and can be worn at the belt.

Belt boxes also are available for carrying worms, grubs, sand maggots, etc.

Refer to the section on Live Shrimp in chapter 4 for instructions on how to keep shrimp alive without water.

Full storm suit

RAINWEAR

Early in anyone's fishing career, he discovers two things—first, he is going to get attacked regularly by rain, spray or fog; second, ordinary raincoats afford little protection—next to none at all in really heavy weather.

The three types of rainwear shown on these pages are the most frequently chosen by active outdoorsmen for the best possible protection from the elements.

The short parka is excellent for use in combination with waders. It extends below the waist, over the top of the waders, and the drawstring can be tightened against chilly updrafts.

The most complete protection is the full storm suit, especially when worn atop rubber boots.

An excellent compromise is the parka. This gives overall protection when worn with hip boots. Even without the boots it is adequate for warm-weather use—keeping most of your body dry, although you get wet below the knees. A shorter, waist-length version of the parka is often worn with waders.

All three styles are obtainable either in inexpensive vinyl, more expensive PVC or expensive waterproofed fabrics. Though welcome in a pinch, the vinyl ones tear easily and are much hotter to wear. Good raingear is worth its price.

MARKER FLOATS

All boating anglers can benefit from keeping a pre-rigged marker float—or perhaps several of them—at hand for quick use. A float is extremely valuable for marking a particular productive spot you might locate, or for orientation in drift-fishing. You may drift for long periods with little or no luck, then suddenly start hitting some fish. Throw over the marker, and you will then be able to circle updrift of it and go back over the productive area repeatedly. It can be surprisingly difficult to retrace your same drifting course without such a marker, because a boat seldom drifts directly downwind, as it might seem—particularly in salt water, where currents may be involved.

In smooth, shallow water, your marker need be nothing more than a regular fishing float with light line and light sinker. The choppier the surface and the deeper the water, the larger your marker should be for visibility. A good choice for coastal fishing is a half-gallon bleach jug. Tie some discarded fishing line to the jug's grip, and wrap enough of the line around the jug to reach bottom in your fishing area—with an ample amount of extra line, or "scope" allowed. A large snap at the end of the line will allow you to affix a heavy sinker, or a piece of scrap metal of suitable weight, to the line. When you want to mark a spot, just toss over the jug. The sinking weight will spin the jug and unwrap the line automatically. When stowage space is a problem, and visibility not so bad, you can use a one-quart plastic bottle instead of the jug.

Lake fishermen can make excellent use of a series of small floats—either manufactured offerings, plastic bottles or fishing bobbers—for marking contours on the lake bottom, such as the course of an old stream bed, or a submerged point or long ledge.

FISH SCALERS

With many species of fish, scaling presents no problem at all. The scales are small, soft and can be flicked away with light pressure of a pocket knife, or even a table knife.

Most members of the sunfish family—bluegills and crappie, for instance—are easily scaled. One especially nifty scaling device for those and other soft-scaled varieties is simply a garden hose. Use a restricting nozzle, turn the pressure up full and direct the flow of water "against the grain" while you hold a fish in your hand. If you have a big string of panfish to scale, the hose works wonders.

Saltwater fish are extremely variable in their willingness to give up their scales. A few, such as weakfish, are as quickly scaled as most freshwater fish. Others, such as red drum, are very tough. In general, saltwater varieties require more scaling effort, and you should not use a knife, because there's a strong chance the blade will slip, or will catch and skid, and give you a nasty cut. Simple scaling devices, of which one of many is pictured here should be employed for heavy work. In a pinch, with no scaler handy, use the edge of a tablespoon.

You may, of course, wish to skin your fish rather than scale them. This is largely a matter of personal preference and experience with various kinds of fish. Many fish are much better when scaled and prepared with the skin left on. A few should always be skinned because the skin contains a "muddy" flavor. This is true of largemouth bass taken from most still, murky waters. While panfish generally are their sweetest when scaled, very large panfish taken from mud-bottomed lakes can definitely be improved by skinning.

Vic's Latest Knowledge Will Help You Catch 'em

This new edition is a major encore for Vic Dunaway, whose byline has been known to anglers all over the country, and in foreign lands as well, for more than 40 years. He has written hundreds of articles for national and regional magazines, and thousands of newspaper columns. He is, of course, a book author and also has appeared on four different television networks, as well as numerous local and syndicated programs.

Though skilled in many different angling specialties, and many writing styles, his strongest interest is in the teaching of fishing skills and enjoyment. Perhaps no other fishing writer has his knack for selecting just the right information on a particular angling subject and presenting it in the quickest, clearest manner—without unnecessary frills or padding.

Dunaway was founding editor when publisher Karl Wickstrom began *Florida Sportsman* Magazine more than a quarter of a century ago, and has played a leading role in the publication's growth into the largest and most authoritative monthly fishing magazine in the country.

FS BOOKS

Published by Florida Sportsman Magazine
2700 S. Kanner Hwy.
Stuart, FL 34994
www.floridasportsman.com/books